PRACTICAL PAINTING

RONALD PEARSALL

CONTENTS

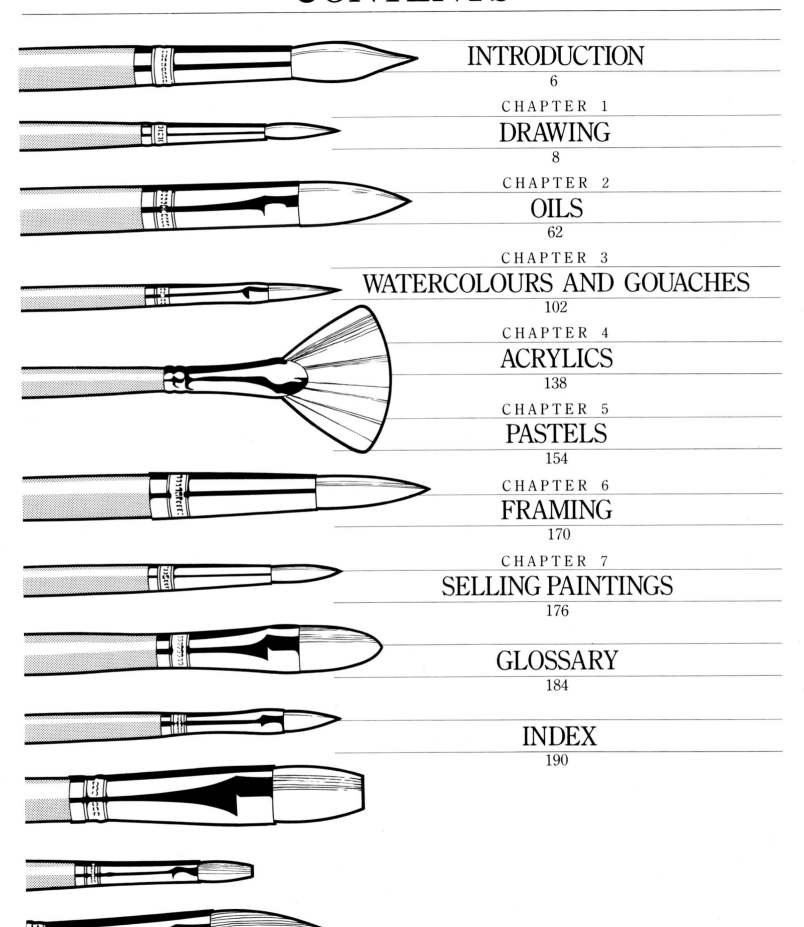

INTRODUCTION

WHY DO PEOPLE PAINT?

There can be only one reason. It is the most absorbing occupation of all, an endless voyage of discovery, a constant quest for new skills and techniques. It is far more than a hobby; it would be impertinent to call it a pastime. As you get better it becomes more and more fascinating; and unlike many hobbies, you do get better. There are not many rugby players or ice-skaters at 50; there are not many chess players who are not past their peak at 40. At 40 many artists are merely beginning to find themselves.

Painting is as easy as you want it to be – or as hard. If you do not want to experiment, you do not have to; if you want to paint garden gnomes you can do this. If you want to try out all the possibilities you have an immense range of materials – oils, acrylic, watercolours, pastels, pen-and-ink, and so on. Whereas the quality of life in some ways has got worse, this is not the case with painting materials. There is a greater range of products in the art shops than there was 30 years ago.

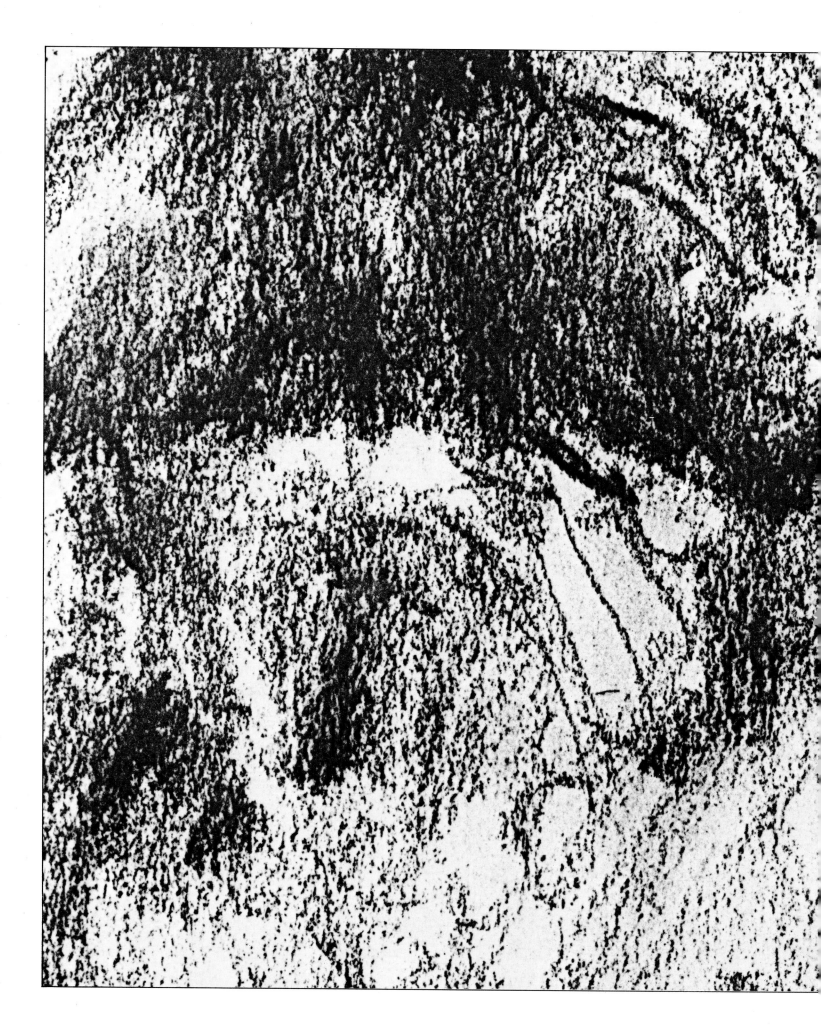

CHAPTER 1

DRAWING

WHAT IS A DRAWING?

The dictionary defines drawing as the art of representing objects or forms by lines drawn, shading, and other means, that is a picture in lines. There are actually at least four types of drawing: trying to represent something in front of the artist; trying to depict something from memory; copying something in another medium; and creating something entirely from imagination. Drawing is usually carried out with a pencil or a pen, charcoal or a crayon, but it can also be done with a pointed instrument on metal (etching) or stone (lithography) or with something soft and flexible such as a brush.

WHAT MATERIALS ARE NEEDED?

Pencils range from the very hard (designated by H) to the very soft and black (B). There are 10 grades between 6B and 4H, the average office pencil being HB. Pencil lead is a mixture of clay and graphite, and the greater the proportion of graphite the softer and blacker the pencil mark. It is useful to have several grades of pencil for use in one drawing. Hard pencils can be sharpened with a pencil-sharpener, but 2B and upwards need to be sharpened with a knife. The point can be tapered or given a chisel edge (very useful for shading). Pencils should always be sharpened at the opposite end to that which shows the degree of hardness or softness; otherwise HB, 2B or 2H or whatever will be lost. Small pieces of sandpaper will keep the pencil point exactly as you want it; art shops sell these in little blocks. There is also an excellent range of coloured pencils in a multitude of shades, but there is little variety of hardness and softness, save between the products of the various manufacturers. These should not be confused with pastel pencils.

Pens also offer an immense range. Drawing-pen nibs are usually sold in sets of a dozen or so, and nibs themselves vary in size from mapping-pen nibs to those designed for doing posters. The larger nibs often come fitted with a kind of a tray, called a reservoir, so that there is a ready flow of ink. Lettering pens can be very useful, and so can the so-called calligraphic pens. Some people refer to pen-nibs as pens, which can be very confusing. For those who find it tiresome to dip the pen in the ink constantly there are of course fountain pens, especially those with interchangeable nib units. Just as the steel nib replaced the quill, so today the steel-nibbed pen has been partly superseded by the rapidograph, which has a range of nibs from 0.1 (very fine) to 0.8 (broad). The virtue of a constant flow of ink and a consistent line compensates for a lack of flexibility in the nib itself. A drawn line cannot be varied by pressing down on the point, as with the old-fashioned steel nib. Rapidographs with a very fine nib do have a tendency to get clogged up, and the nibs need a good deal of care.

Inks come in numerous colours, though black remains the most popular. Indian ink is probably the best kind of ink to use. Ink can be waterproof and water-soluble, and coloured inks can be used to great effect in combination with watercolour, especially on a moist surface where the colours can run into each other. Ordinary dip-in ink should never be used in a rapidograph pen, and there is no chance of doing this by accident as rapidograph ink is supplied in containers with a special filler to fill the rapidograph cartridge.

Papers Anything which will take a pen or pencil line can be used for drawing. Artists of the past showed a particular fondness for the backs of old envelopes. The traditional art-school paper is cartridge paper, sold in various weights, and best bought in sheet form and cut in two or four. Decent cartridge paper takes watercolour well, and is a good substitute for watercolour paper as well as being less expensive. Tinted papers, such as Ingres pastel paper, take pencil, pen and ink well, but almost anything can be used, though much depends on whether you are playing about with ideas, doing preliminary drawings, or are going to spend time on a finished pencil drawing good enough to frame. Sketchbooks are very handy, especially for on-the-spot work outdoors, as they usually have a thick cardboard back.

Drawing-board The best drawing-boards are keyed, battened and proofed against warping and shrinking and all the other ailments wood is prone to. The most useful attribute of the drawing-board is that it takes drawing-pins, which alternatives such as a piece of hardboard will not. A drawing-board of the traditional kind can be very useful in a life class where the drawing is on a vertical easel. A proper drawing-board has just the right amount of give to a pencil point; a substitute may be too hard and shiny. Some people prefer to tape their drawings to a board with sellotape or masking tape (preferable, as it is easier to strip off the paper edge).

Easel Often looked on as an optional extra, an easel, especially a small portable one, can come in very handy, even for drawing. In out-of-doors situations it is often a good thing to stand back from the picture to see how it is going. Some artists never use an easel at all, even for doing oils, so it is very much a personal choice. Drawing at a vertical angle is altogether different from drawing on the flat or on a slope.

Erasers There are three kinds of pencil erasers on the market: putty rubbers, which can be very tiresome and crumble up into black pellets but which are ultra-soft and good for toning down blacks; the traditional office-type eraser; and the plastic type which has largely taken over from the second

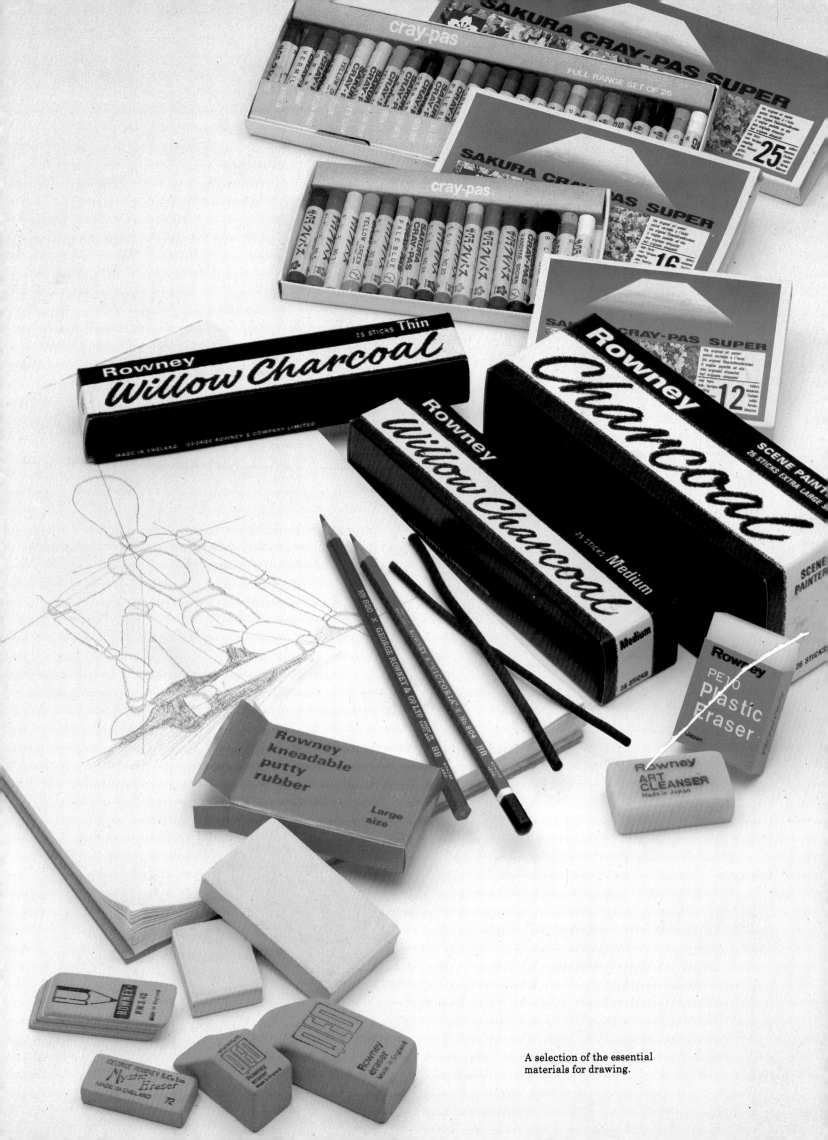

A selection of the essential materials for drawing.

group as it is 'clean' and very versatile.

Charcoal At one time every art student wielded a stick of charcoal in the life class, and it has much to commend its use. It produces a soft black, which is easy to rub out even with a finger tip. However it is not very suitable for fine detail and students are inclined to work on a larger scale than they would do with a pencil. This was considered a good thing by art masters, who had a paranoiac fear of niggardly work. Used on its side, it is very good for blocking in shadows, rather than hatching them in with a pencil.

Torchon or Stump These are pencil-shaped articles of compressed blotting-paper or similar material, used for spreading charcoal, or cleaning up edges, and also useful in pen-and-ink work where they can tone down colours or blot out mistakes. Cotton-wool buds as sold in chemists can also be used in charcoal work or pen-and-ink.

Of course there are other accessories to add to the basic materials if and when wanted. A toothbrush is often used in pen-and-ink work to 'spatter' ink on to a surface, and sometimes drawings develop into watercolours or pastels, so it is always handy to have the necessary equipment nearby.

Far left: A selection of different papers used for drawing, showing how the different finishes and textures affect the character of the drawing.

Far left: A characteristic study of a nude girl, carried out freely and spontaneously.

The various grades of blackness achieved by pencils from 4H to 8B, charcoal pencil and chinagraph pencil.

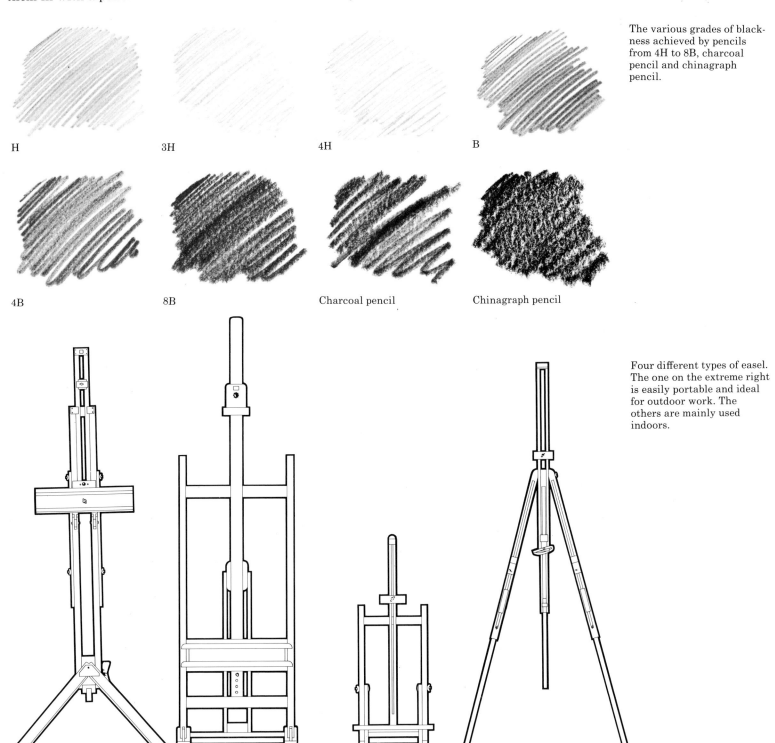

H

3H

4H

B

4B

8B

Charcoal pencil

Chinagraph pencil

Four different types of easel. The one on the extreme right is easily portable and ideal for outdoor work. The others are mainly used indoors.

IS DRAWING DIFFICULT?

Learning to draw is like learning to play the piano, only easier. The classic form of drawing is reproducing something in front of you, whether it be a bunch of grapes, a nude or a landscape. In the art schools of yesteryear there was no chance of you touching a paint-brush until you could do this. This is the reason artists of the past were very accomplished; whether they were imaginative or at all interesting is another matter. The first thing to do if you are drawing from life is to forget what you know; you are drawing what an object looks like, not what it is – unless, of course, you do not want to be representational, in which case you can draw what you like.

It is interesting to speculate on why prehistoric man made his cave drawings of animals. The most commonly accepted theory was these drawings were a form of magic, and that by depicting animals with spears in them he would be rewarded with success in the hunt. To the professional artists of the Middle Ages and after art was for the glory of God. When they painted Jesus and the Madonna they were not concerned with where the shadows went. Putting in a halo of gold leaf was more important than verisimilitude. Coming up to the present day, and ignoring for the moment that the Romans and the Egyptians could put down *exactly* on panels and walls what they saw, we can see in children's art the wish to put down on paper what they know rather than what they see. A circle with two blobs, a vertical stroke, and a crescent shape at the bottom is a face, and a rectangle with four squares, an oblong, and another oblong at the top exuding smoke, represents a house (even for those in tower blocks who only see a house once in a blue moon).

Some people, including artists, never lose this way of looking at objects, or, rather, pretend not to have lost it. The childish vision allied with a solid technique can often be a money-spinner. Art teachers are usually the first to try to eradicate the child's way of depicting external objects, and place before the class cubes and spheres and other dreary objects. No wonder that many children do not find much fun in drawing.

The child's way of drawing is to put down an outline and then colour the bits enclosed. This is an instinctive way and adults will do much the same without thinking about it, though if you reflect a little you will realize that an outline does not exist 'out there'. An outline is only a dividing line between an area of light and an area somewhat darker. In other words, an outline is a convention. It is a convention that in drawing all artists will continue to respect – though not in painting, where changes in *tone* (not colour) are all important.

In drawing, except using coloured pencils or coloured inks, all we have is outline and tone. Our aim is to depict with reasonable accuracy what we see. Success does not depend on manual dexterity.

Prehistoric wall paintings, which can be interpreted in many ways, as magic or maybe as reminders of successful missions. There is no question about their immediacy and verve.

It depends on looking and assessing. By assessing we mean simply seeing how certain shapes relate to other shapes and how light or dark they are in respect of each other. Sometimes the shapes are simple, and can be looked at once and set down with something like accuracy. In landscape it can be a farmhouse set against a field. Sometimes the shapes are complex, such as the angle of a wrist in a life drawing. No shape is too difficult to put down. We do not have to know how the farm was built and its methods of interior construction. Nor do we have to be anatomists to find out why the wrist turns in one way and no other, though it is only fair to mention that artists of the old school needed to be well versed in anatomy (and sometimes robbed graveyards for specimens to dissect). These are the principles behind drawing, and after a time it becomes second nature to recreate on paper the external appearance of something. The next stage is using the drawing, either as a basis for something else, or as a spur to further composition.

Once we realize that the outline is only a means to an end and that the effect of *solidity* is far more important than a pencil line surrounding a white silhouette, then the main barrier to accurate drawing is crossed. This may sound daunting for some, who believe that they will never be any good at

Children sometimes draw in outlines and then colour the space between, and this technique is often used by artists including Patrick Cauldfield. The detail (*below*) from his delightful painting also exemplifies the use of perspective; the tops of the pots go from the nearly circular to the horizontal, where the pots are seen at eye level, and beyond.

A fully worked drawing of a train. Trains are extremely complicated things to draw and it requires much patience and observation to achieve a drawing like this.

drawing. Useful as the skill is, drawing is not the be all and end all. It is quite possible to be a bad draughtsman yet a good painter. There are a large number of short cuts that can be taken, and there is no need for anyone to ever bother drawing something from life if they do not feel confident about it, though it must be said that although it is a kind of discipline it is great fun, and it is fascinating to see a drawing gradually emerge from the first marks made on the paper, whether it is a bit of shading, a few squiggles to mark where the shapes come, or a fragment of line.

Before we pursue the practical side of drawing, a few words on the subject of perspective.

Perspective

Perspective is a simple matter. If you look at a straight road going towards the horizon it appears to narrow; a person walking along this road appears to get smaller as the distance increases between you and the other person, losing height at the same rate as the road narrows. Telegraph poles will appear to shrink. If the road extends as far as the eye can see, the sides will appear to meet at what is known as the vanishing point on the horizon. The horizon is *always* at eye-level, and to prove it, sit or lie on the ground and watch how the horizon goes down with you. The horizon has *nothing* to do with the sky-line, and the only time to observe a true horizon is at sea where the sky meets the water.

Objects above or partly above the eye-level *appear* to go down towards the horizon and those below *appear* to go up. If you look at the roof of a house from any angle except directly in front, you will see it obeying the laws of perspective. If you extend the roof with an imaginary line it will lead to the horizon at its own particular vanishing point. There is only one horizon line, but there can be any number of vanishing points in any one scene. Without using perspective, a drawing or a painting will be flat, a mere pattern. Using perspective you get solidity and recession; you can place things in space with absolute certainty that you are getting the relative sizes right, because everything fits into the pattern.

In working from the imagination, the horizon can be as high or low as you wish. If you are doing aerial views it can even be off the top of the paper. But objects still recede towards it according to the rules. The laws of perspective must be used. Use perspective to help establish objects in space, and twist it if you need to get a better effect. The experts in perspective drawing are not usually artists, but architects. Their perspective has to be absolutely right, but if an artist's perspective *looks* right, that is what matters. It is easy to imagine roads, roofs, and telegraph poles going

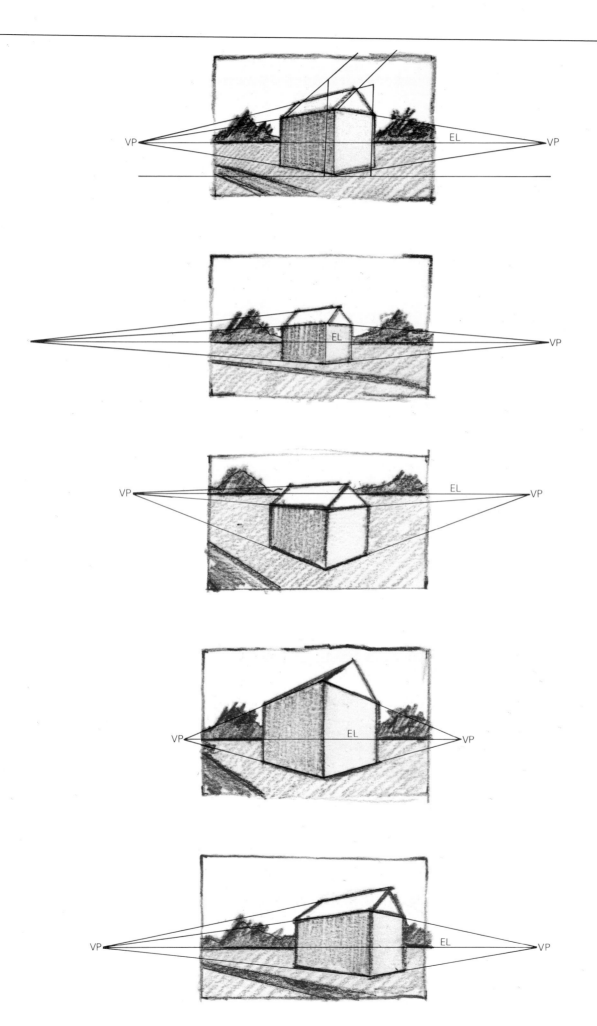

Left: These five sketches of a hut illustrate the way in which perspective alters according to the eye level (EL) and viewpoint. When the viewpoint is far away, the angle of perspective is very shallow and the vanishing points (VP) from both walls fall some distance away. As the viewpoint becomes nearer, the vanishing points close up, and the angle of perspective becomes much sharper.

Right: It is important when drawing or painting buildings to ensure that the perspective is accurate. Always sketch the basic perspective before adding detail and colour. Modern architecture with its clean line and form often demonstrates perspective at its most uncompromising and is good practice.

conveniently towards vanishing points. Asymmetrical objects such as oval-shaped ponds also obey the laws of perspective, and no one in their right mind wants to work out *exactly* how perspective works on them. If you are drawing from life, you can see; if you are not, but would like to put in an oval pond somewhere, you put one in and see if it looks right.

A brief mention should be made of accidental vanishing points. Surfaces which are tilted (academically described as 'surfaces which are inclined to the horizontal') *sometimes* converge on accidental vanishing points which lie above or below the horizon – and not on it. A good example of this is a road going uphill, where the sides will appear to converge at a point *above* the horizon, vice versa in the case of a road going downhill. This fact is another reason not to be too much in awe of so-called laws.

There is a useful tip: an object twice as far away from the viewer as another identical object appears to be half as tall; if it is three times as far away it seems one-third as tall; four times as far away, a quarter as tall, and so on. Another useful tip is: even in good drawings and paintings the clouds sometimes seem flat and uninteresting. This is because clouds are also subject to the laws of perspective.

Aerial perspective, oddly enough, does not have anything to do with ordinary perspective. You might think it means aerial views, and how objects on the ground have vanishing points outside the picture surface (or, if seen from directly above, have no vanishing point at all!) This is not the case. Aerial perspective is the effect of atmosphere. Atmosphere is full of moisture, dust, not to mention noxious fumes, which tend to obscure the most distant objects. The more distant objects are, the more they are obscured, and the lighter or higher in tone they will appear to be. Distant features often take on a bluish tone, and 18th-century artists had a formula that was worked to death – dark brown for the foreground, green for the middle distance and blue for the far distance. This became a device for achieving a good effect without much soul-searching. In the early morning, distant objects can be as crisp and un-blue as you care to imagine. So aerial perspective is something we can take or leave, depending on the effect we want.

HOW DO I START?

In most cases, it is not a question of starting but of continuing. Most people have drawn at some time in their life, even if it is only a doodle on a telephone pad. The main question is: do I want a challenge or do I want to take the easy way? The challenge is to do *something* from real life and get professional or amateur opinion on your drawing as the work progresses – in other words, join an art class or a sketching club.

Lessons at art classes are cheap, especially if

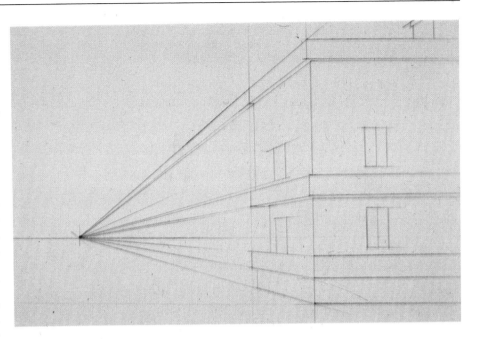

A photograph of a boat, and a spin-off showing the use of the 'squaring-up' technique in the form of an illustration. The usefulness of a collection of photographs and illustrations of all kinds cannot be over-emphasized.

they are run by the local council. The ultimate challenge for beginners is to join a life class, and paint the nude figure. The models in life classes have to stand still and be drawn or painted, which is actually very hard work. If you are worried about not being good enough for the class, do not. Most adults who go to life classes are *not* very good at drawing, and some of them never will be because they find going to a life class enjoyable as a night out and because of the people they meet there. Many of them do not particularly want to improve, and others do not take kindly to any form of instruction from the teachers, who consequently have to be masters of tact and diplomacy (and usually are – the traditional stuffy ones are a dying breed).

Sketching clubs are usually concerned with landscape, which is easier than life drawing (in this context life is drawing from the nude). Experienced artists often go with sketching clubs, for the sake of companionship and comfort. For those sociably inclined, there is a lot to be said for sketching clubs, which usually include experienced artists as well as learners. There is no easier way to pick up techniques and tips almost by accident. Overlooking a good artist at work can be very rewarding, and it is amazing, by simply looking around, how many styles and methods of drawing and painting there are.

Drawing at home, watched occasionally by a husband or wife, father or mother, or, more unnerving, children, may or may not be more acceptable, but it is important to give yourself something of a challenge. Do not spend too much time drawing something which bores you to distraction; if you feel that you ought to try a still life, set up an interesting group, and if the drawing is going badly finish it quickly and turn to something else which is more stimulating, whether it be the dog curled up on a carpet, a self-portrait, or a view from a window. There is no obligation to do pretty or picturesque subjects, nor any of those tiresome exercises middle-aged men and women remember from their school days. If it is not enjoyable it is not worth doing; nobody is paying you, and if it becomes a chore you might as well settle down in front of the television screen.

The whole emphasis of this book is on pleasure. If you would like to go out with a sketchbook but feel that you will look foolish, go in the car and stay in the car while you sketch. You do not *have* to set up in the open air with all the paraphernalia associated with a 'real artist'. If you feel that you will never be any good at drawing but want to paint, do not despair. There are any number of short cuts which will enable you to set down some kind of 'drawing' as a basis for painting, whatever the paint medium.

One of the greatest aids to artists is a collection of illustrations, photographs, photographs of people, landscapes, seascapes, prize-winning photographs, photographs in books and catalogues, snapshots, polaroids and photographs of pictures, to mention only a few examples. Most artists of the past accumulated illustrations; be-

fore the 1840s they were prints and paintings; between 1840 and about 1880 photographs were added to the collection, but these photographs were 'one-offs' as no way had been found to reproduce photographs in books except by sticking them in with gum. These photographs were all monochrome; colour photographs were not developed for a long time. Today colour photographs are available, and have been for a quarter of a century. They form a valuable source of information, though black-and-white photographs can be even more useful as an aid because they deal with tone, which to an artist is more informative than colour.

Photographs can be consulted, and for those for whom drawing is their weak point, they can be copied – or even traced. If all you want is a basis for a picture, not a drawing to be proud of, there is much to be said for tracing. There is no need to trace an entire photograph – just the elements you want. Photographs can always be copied, and an advantage of copying is that the replica can be executed on a larger scale than the original by 'squaring-up'. Squaring-up is a traditional way of transferring a preliminary drawing on to a canvas, and all it means is that the drawing and the canvas are divided into squares. The numbers of squares on the drawing and the canvas are the same, but as the drawing is usually smaller the squares on the canvas need to be larger. The same can be done with a photograph. Originals can also be copied, larger or smaller, by using a device called a pantograph, which is something like a flat wine-rack with interchangeable struts, a pointer to follow the lines of the original, and a pencil at the opposite end of the device for reproducing the picture. If you do buy a pantograph get a good one, and not a cheap plastic type which is no better than an irritating toy.

Using the squaring-up method it is simple to copy the material contained in each square, ensuring that the proportions are correct, which is vitally important in figure and portrait work. Many of the great painters of the past have used this method, and it is wholly acceptable. More artists than you might imagine have used tracing as a basis for transferring designs onto paper or canvas. The only problem with tracing is that unless one has a darkroom and photographic ability (or a good deal of money) photographic prints are relatively small, except in 'coffee-table' books, a source of illustration not to be overlooked. It is amazing how you can build up a picture using various photographs, even though it means altering the light and shade.

Among the most useful photographs are those you have taken yourself. A photograph not only jogs the memory, but is also valuable as a record; it can replace a sketch done on the spot for working-up later into a picture, or it can supplement a sketch. Using a polaroid camera as one is sketching can be very rewarding, bringing out features in landscape which you have overlooked, and establishing the exact look of a place, as well as the general colour and tone. Few professional por-

trait artists work without recourse to a number of photographs of their sitters. Using a camera can, if desired, do away with preliminary drawing.

So far we have been dealing with photographic *prints* as an aid to or a substitute for drawing, but colour transparencies can also serve a purpose. They are not so easy to flip through in search of subjects or information, but unquestionably they have their place. The image on a transparency is, of course, thrown onto a screen. Provided that you keep out of the way of the light source and substitute paper or canvas for the screen there is no problem in painting the picture as it is being projected. Painting-by-numbers with a difference. It is the procedure of highly regarded artists of the neo-realist school in the USA, and is no more reprehensible than collage, the use of silk-screen printing, and the innumerable dodges of contemporary art. If it suits you, and you like doing it, do it.

A casual mention must be made of video as an aid to artists. It cannot be used directly, but it can be a valuable source of information on every sub-

When making a tracing it is important not only to put in outline but shading as well.

Tracing the image.

Following the lines on the reverse side.

Retracing the lines.

ject. In the old days an artist who wanted to study the sea and analyse the structure and pattern of waves had to go to the sea to look at it. If you are keen on doing maritime pictures, you will always find television scenes involving the sea, even if it is in the middle of a feature film. Such a section can be played over and over again, with certain episodes frozen to see exactly what waves look like. In today's world we can find out about almost everything without needing to go out-of-doors. How documentary-type artists of the past would have envied us!

Copying, tracing and reproducing are all short-cuts to painting, bypassing the process of drawing and the co-ordination of hand and eye. No one is going to award you a prize for diligently slogging away at a drawing when you are not really enjoying it, and if you happen to turn out a good painting very few are likely to enquire about the initial techniques you used. Copying, using the squaring-up method or freehand, needs little said about it; for tracing one needs a pad of proper tracing-paper as sold by art shops, not too thick and not too flimsy. When tracing put in the tones as well as the outlines. There are two main methods of transferring the tracing paper or canvas, first, by using carbon paper. This is all right when using opaque watercolour or oils, but in watercolour proper the carbon lines are too dark and do not rub out easily. The second is going over the lines on the reverse side of the tracing paper with charcoal or soft pencil, then applying the tracing paper right way up and going over the detail with a hard pencil (HB or H) or a ball-point pen. Charcoal has the slight edge on pencil as it is easily removed or obliterated by almost any medium from the lightest watercolour upwards. If there is a slight disadvantage with charcoal it is that the image can be a little 'fluffy'.

Let us suppose that you have not taken the easy option and are willing to draw something in front of you. Whatever you are drawing, you must decide whether to stand at an easel or sit down. If you are sitting down, you can have your drawing-board or sketchpad on your knees, or on a table. If you are sitting down and want to work on a vertical surface but have not got an easel, two dining-chairs tied together by the front legs make an excellent substitute, sitting on one and resting the drawing-board on the back of the other. Large-scale work is better done standing up, as the action comes from the shoulder rather than the wrist so there is a greater freedom.

The way you hold the pencil is a question of taste; in writing it is held between the thumb and the first or second finger. In drawing, try holding the pencil with all four fingers beneath it, thumb on top, and knuckles against the paper. This is for standing up. For sitting down, reverse the procedure, and in both cases it will give you flexibility if you hold the pencil loosely and not too near the point. For pen-and-ink work it is also worthwhile trying new pen holds.

In drawing any object, establish roughly what you are going to put in. In a still life, it is quite simple; you make the arrangement, so you put it all in. In a nude you will *try* to get it all in, but sometimes the odd ankle somehow does not fit into the picture. Landscape has to be cut off somewhere, and you may decide to put the most interesting features somewhere in the middle and let the rest take care of itself. Alternatively, you can make use of a view-finder, which you can make yourself out of a piece of card, and is nothing more or less than a small picture mount with a convenient-size rectangle cut into a piece of larger card. A camera view-finder can be useful. In portrait drawing obviously the whole of the face must go in, and the rest you can leave rough or finished as you wish.

The very first step is to get *something* down on the virgin paper. There is nothing more demanding than an empty piece of paper. You may like to put in a few light touches indicating the size and position of the subject, or you may care to start by indicating with the flat of the charcoal or by hatching with a series of parallel lines the areas of shadow. If they are wrong, it does not matter, do not rub them out. As you get more certain that you are on the right track, the lines and shadows can get firmer and more authoritative. Fashion designers usually put in the entire outlines, and then fill them in. If you have a good eye, you can do this but it is normally only possible with practice. It is usually easier to move from point to point, from drawing fragments you are reasonably satisfied with, whether they are bits of outline or areas of shade, to new sections.

In the early stages it is very easy to come adrift on questions of proportion. A pencil held at arm's length is very helpful; the distance between point A and point B can be equated between the tip of the pencil and the top of the thumb nail. There is nothing to stop you using a 12 in wooden ruler for this task. Divergences from the vertical and the horizontal can also be figured out with the help of a pencil held at arm's length. It is easier to underestimate an angle than over-estimate it.

Shadows come in all shapes and sizes, and because we are not really used to examining shadows, there are more varieties than we might imagine. There are shadows arising from the object part being away from the light source, there are background shadows, and there are cast shadows, in which one object is shielding another object or part object from the light. Cast shadows are darker than other shadows. If there is more than one light source, the shadows can be very interesting, and you may have to decide which ones you want and which you do not. The usual way to draw in shadow is to hatch it, but you can also use dots or scribbles; for strong shadow you can use cross-hatch, in which parallel strokes from right diagonally down to the left (or vice versa if you are left-handed) are overlaid by parallel strokes top left to down right. Or if you are using a soft pencil with a chisel point you can put the shadow in solid black. Try to build up the drawing with a combination of outline and shading; they complement each other. This applies to all types of drawing.

There are many ways of holding the pencil or other drawing implement, and you will find the method which suits you best.

General sketching work.

Shading large areas.

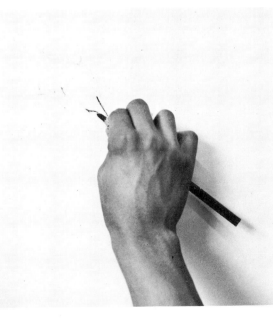

Detail work.

If you are setting up a still life at home or are drawing a husband or wife you can decide for yourself what source of light you want. The only advice is not to have the light source immediately behind the subject. A room with windows on one side only provides more comprehensible shadows than a room with several light sources; for really direct shadows, there is nothing better than electric light, with an unshielded standard lamp or anglepoise lamp better than an overhead bulb or fluorescent.

In landscapes we have to depend on the sun, and if we are interested in drawing for drawing's sake it is better to go out when the light is good, as well as in the early morning or late afternoon when the shadows are at their most interesting. Needless to say, there are no hard or fast rules about this; atmospheric drawings can be made on occasions when a photographer would hardly get a reading on his light-meter.

HAVING STARTED THE DRAWING, HOW DO I CARRY ON?

Your drawing may at this stage look like tea leaves in the bottom of a tea cup or automatic writing at a spiritualist seance. It does not matter if you have bits of outlines and areas of shading as long as you have an idea, however vague, what is going on and are not merely putting in strokes and blobs at random. It is more important that you can see a way to get to grips with the subject, and can assess it as a whole, knowing from which direction the light is coming and what are going to be the stumbling blocks which need extra effort. If you find it difficult to work out the tones, and cannot decide which areas should be darker, half-close your eyes and look at the subject again.

Every drawing exercise has its difficult aspects, and sometimes it is a good idea to tackle these separately, on a separate sheet of paper or on the corner. In still life, it may be the curvature on jugs or bowls and how to put in the graded shading as the curve moves into the dark, or it may be that you are tackling a vase of flowers and wondering how to manage those flowers partly in the shadow of blooms above them. In landscape, it may be the problem of depicting trees so that they do not look like overgrown cabbages. In life drawing, a common disaster area is the hand and wrist, and even great artists can come unstuck. In portraits, you may have a problem in preventing the subject looking cross-eyed. Each of us has a particular area which we find fraught with difficulty, even if there is no sensible reason why this should be so. However you must persevere and try to crack it. If a hand looks like a melon, rub it out and start again, though it may be that you have already gone over it a dozen times and the lines and indentations are beyond redemption. If the rest of the

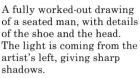
A fully worked-out drawing of a seated man, with details of the shoe and the head. The light is coming from the artist's left, giving sharp shadows.

drawing is going well, it is much more convenient to paste a piece of paper over the offending part and carry on over that (adhesive envelope labels – they used to be called 'economy labels' – are ideal for this purpose).

There is no substitute for looking *hard* at something which is proving intractable, and this is where a photographic collection can be invaluable. Examine what the difficult object *really* looks like and how painters and draughtsmen of the past have managed to make their efforts believable. It is sometimes a good idea, even if you are a dedicated non-copier, to copy a detail from another picture and in so doing realize where you went wrong. Many of the problems of drawing derive from the fact that you are trying to interpret a three-dimensional object in two dimensions, and that parts of an object are nearer to you than others, sometimes quite dramatically. This is most evident in life drawing, and *foreshortening*. Imagine a fist extended towards your face; the knuckles of the hand will take up most of the image, and the shoulder at the back will be very insignificant indeed. Sometimes problems will fall away if we remember about perspective, and that *everything* is set in space and is subject to its laws. Even in a still life it is sometimes helpful to put in an eye-line, and insert vanishing points.

There is nothing more rewarding than working away through your own personal drawing problem, but here are some tips to make it easier.

Figure Drawing

It is traditional in old-fashioned teach-yourself books to emphasize that beneath clothing is a nude and beneath the nude is a skeleton, not to mention muscles. There is nothing more offputting than anatomy. As we are not going to draw skeletons, we can take it as read that they are there and influence the shape and movements of the body. The proportions of the various sections are much more useful. A man is eight heads tall, a woman six heads; bearing in mind the fact that we are all different, the half-way point down a man is the crutch or thereabouts. Some professional artists and fashion designers have the women at eight-and-a-half heads tall, with longer legs than is natural (or often seen). A one-year-old child is four heads high; a nine-year-old child is six heads tall. Regarding the shape of the torso, that of a man, broad of shoulder and narrow of hip, can be represented by an equilateral triangle upright from a tip, that of a woman by a triangle on one of its sides. Tricky areas for novices are connecting the head with the shoulders in a convincing manner, the hands and the feet. The neck, unless the head is thrown back, tilts forward; a man's neck slopes slightly *outwards*, a woman's neck slightly *inwards*. The neck does not stick on *top* of the shoulders, but is slightly below. A fist is harder to draw, though there is less of it, than an outstretched hand, and always be aware of the angle and relative smallness of the wrist. You can practise drawing your own hand, preferably with the aid of a mirror. It is far more important to get

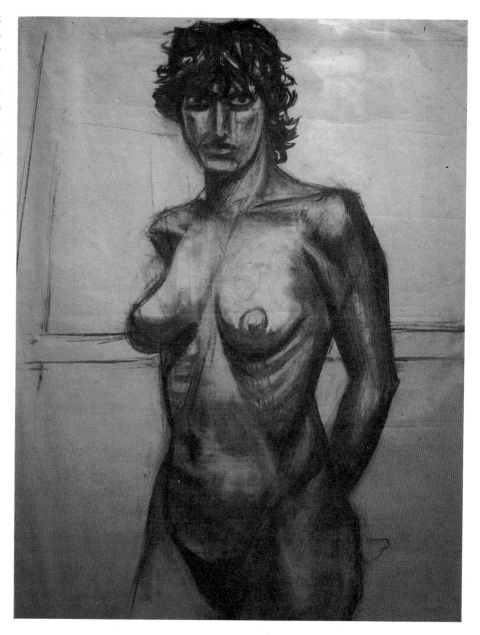

Above: It is important, when drawing the figure, to have an understanding of how the body is formed and how various parts are joined. In this study of a nude, the artist has shown that he understands the structure of the body with its clearly defined bone structure.

Detail of the head.

A reclining nude. When doing a drawing of a figure at this angle, there can be problems with foreshortening.

A powerful study of a man. Here, the artist has gone for atmosphere and feeling rather than realism, but without losing the form. The shading on the left has been achieved by rubbing over a rough wooden surface.

A fully worked study of a couple. The drapes and folds of the clothes have been particularly well drawn. Remember that clothes generally follow the form of the body.

A quick charcoal sketch of a
seated couple. It is a good
idea to practise drawing
people in your home, when
they are watching television,
or reading, or even in the
bath!

In this drawing of a reclining
nude, the artist has chosen
to define form by light and
shade rather than by line.
Here, the charcoal has been
rubbed with a finger to
achieve the soft feel of the
drawing, and a rubber has
been used to obtain
definition.

A strong, angular study in charcoal, where the jutting bone structure of the face is well defined.

Right: Figures in movement can present difficulties, but when these have been overcome the challenges provided can prove very rewarding.

Below: Details of the left arm and legs; these are likely to present the most problems but, with observation, even the most outlandish movements can be set down accurately.

Far right: A fairly standard way of posing the sitter, with the light source behind the artist.

The gradual building-up of a portrait, relating areas of shadow or fragments of line to other areas and lines.

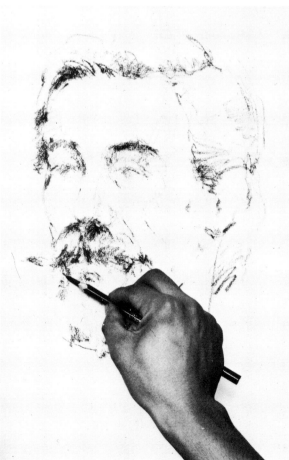

The finished drawing,
achieved in approximately
10 minutes.

contained in a perfect square. If there is any part of an animal that presents difficulties, it is the leg, especially the back leg. The curious shape of a dog's back legs is obvious, but those of other animals are not so straightforward as you might remember. When drawing animals in herds, it is not usually necessary to make a study of each of them. This is more apparent in paintings, where sheep (simple animals to draw) are often represented by landscapists as blobs with a bit of black at one end and four sticks as legs.

Birds are delightful to draw because they have so few component parts, and it is not difficult to relate wing-length to body-length. There is however little point in trying to draw them in real life. The wild-life programmes on television are a boon to bird artists, as they are to all wild-life painters, giving close-ups we would never experience otherwise.

Landscape

Landscape-drawing and painting are among the great pleasures of life, even for those who are just setting out on their artistic career whether 16 or 60. It is easy to get dewy-eyed on the subject of Nature, and we tend to take it for granted, along with Wordsworth and his daffodils. We may look at Nature at its most spectacular if we are told to in a guide-book, but too often it is something we pass on the motorway.

Nature does not move very much, so you can spend as much or as little time drawing one subject as you wish. However, the lighting does change, often dramatically, though this is of more concern to painters than to those who are just using a pencil or pen-and-ink. Shadows change gradually with the passing hours, and not too quickly to put down. Once again it is important that a house is not seen as a rectangle with four squares in for windows, but as a pattern of light and shade. Remember what you are looking at and forget what it is, and watch for groupings. Draw something interesting to *you*, not something which you feel is a right and proper subject for the Artistic with a capital A. If you like bungalows, draw bungalows rather than the parish church. If ordinary landscape bores you, stick to the town – many famous artists have built up their reputations from their pictures of the suburbs.

As with all kinds of art, you have a multitude of choices, not only with the particular view you have selected out of countless options, but whether

Studies of animals. Animals have a tendency to move quickly and suddenly and rarely assume the same positions, so this should be borne in mind when sketching living creatures of all kinds.

The head of a horse. Most animals have longer necks than one might imagine, but painters of the horse in previous times have had a tendency to elongate the neck to ridiculous lengths to give the impression of speed.

The torso and legs of an animal within a square, well illustrated in this drawing of a horse.

whether it is tilted, what happens when it dips. Whereas in much landscape detail we have to forget what we know in order to see accurately, when we are dealing with the surface on which all the features are positioned the only way we know which way the ground is going is by the light and shade we are looking at.

In a drawing (but of course not a painting) the sky and the clouds are of minor importance, and if clouds are put in they should be put in lightly as otherwise their presence will overwhelm what is happening on the ground below. Water in a landscape is always a plus, and the reflections in water can add great interest to a picture. It is necessary to really *look* at reflections, and not put in replicas of what is above the water level. Rippling water makes nonsense of mirror images. There is a weird sort of perspective in reflections, and there is also the question of refraction, in which the reflections do not make sense. It is important to look and digest.

Townscape
Most books on practical painting do not mention townscape, which is a pity because it offers much to those who live in towns and who find the countryside somewhat alien. Although it does not always do to generalize, a townscape is usually simpler to draw and paint than a landscape, especially for those who have come to grips with perspective. You are also not diverted from looking for the differences in light and shade by too

These pen and ink drawings
of elder (*below*) and sorrel
(*right*) show great draughts-
manship. The meticulous
brushwork highlights every
detail to make an exact
reproduction of the plants.
The outline has been drawn
in pale ink and thicker
washes have been used to
fill in the detail.

much colour. Townscapes can merge into landscapes, but the gaunt industrial towns of the north have their own kind of sombre beauty and even, as in the paintings of L. S. Lowry, a wistful charm. Many of the recommendations for country drawing apply to townscapes – do not let the detail in the middle distance get out of hand, draw when there are interesting shadow-shapes about, let the features stand out for themselves and do not over-emphasize important features. Sometimes a townscape looks odd without figures, and although this will not matter much in a drawing which is meant to represent what you are seeing, if the drawing is worked up into a painting figures – inserted according to the rules of perspective – do add interest to a townscape. No need to go mad

with them, as Lowry did. They also serve as splashes of colour in paintings, and are useful for setting the scale of the adjacent buildings and other features. As with traditional landscape, water adds interest; in townscapes it is usually a river or a canal. Many of today's canals are derelict and consequently picturesque – and usually situated in the inner suburbs and run-down areas. What with traffic and hordes of people, it is often advisable to carry a camera with you when searching for townscapes.

When you are adding figures to a landscape or a townscape, always remember that they have shadows which must go the same way as those already in the picture. Shadows can be useful if you are putting in groups of people, and cast

The people and traffic are mere suggestions in this sketch, but the bustle of the street is well conveyed and contrasts nicely against the grandeur of the building behind.

shadows, where one person is standing obscuring or partly obscuring a neighbour, can depict figures as certainly as line. For townscapes to be really believable, they need to contain objects we take for granted and hardly notice are there, for example, cars, moving and parked. As with figures, they often add colour to a picture or an accent in an otherwise empty spot, but if you draw a car from memory you will find it an odd experience. You will probably overemphasize the upper part of the car, which is actually little more than a glass box on top of the solid bodywork. The wheels also pose a problem; how much is hidden under the wings? You need to *look* at cars or have some in your photographic collection.

When drawing cars, shadows are very important, for if there is any light at all the area beneath the wings and the car itself will be in dense shadow. Although it does not matter so much in drawing, the metal of the car will throw off highlights, and in paintings these highlights can be employed very effectively. Drawing cars is a good way of getting to know how to draw other mechanical objects, and coming to terms with circular objects which turn into ellipses as they turn away from us or to us. Whether the angle of the ellipse is *exactly* right is of less importance than the need to keep it symmetrical, and not have odd bulges on one side. By all means use aids to get your wheels right. Stationers keep a stock of stencils of various sized circles and other useful shapes, and these stencils can also be used for ellipses by tracing down one side, and then the other, leaving out the section in the middle and joining the two arcs together by freehand. It will not be a perfect ellipse, but it should prove convincing enough and that is the object of it all – what looks right, is right. If you are putting imaginary cars into a townscape, or, for that matter, a landscape, work out whether the windows will look transparent or opaque. One of the main points to remember about cars is that they are not very high; a man of reasonable height can stand by a car and rest his elbows on the roof. So in a street scene with pedestrians and traffic, pedestrians' heads will always appear well above the roofs of the cars.

Still Life
A drawing of a landscape, townscape, portrait or figure will often stand by itself as a work of art. A still life rarely does. Still-life drawings are usually used as a basis for a painting or as an exercise, and even the most accomplished still-life drawing· is not intrinsically interesting. The one great advantage of still life is that you are in control of the composition, arranging the lighting as you want it, getting the shadows you like, and grouping the objects in the most acceptable manner.

Seascapes
Much of what has been said about landscapes applies to seascapes, and if anything seascapes are easier, provided you put the horizon in *exactly* the horizontal position – otherwise the sea will appear to be slipping downhill. Ships are fine subjects for drawing, but it is better to get them right, for it is incredible how many people know about ships and which way the sails should go and why that mast is two metres (or should it be a furlong?) too tall. In a landscape it does not matter if the tree is the wrong shape; in boats it does.

Boats are usually entities in themselves, and, unlike some landscape features, they make sense, and can be summed up at a glance. Boats in the foreground or tied up together at a quay can also be figured out, even though you may not know what all the ropes are for. The shadows on boats are also comprehensible; if the shadow is on one side of the boat, it will apply to *all* that side, and as the superstructure is usually in one block cast shadows are not much of a problem. Do not get bogged down with all the ropes and lines unless you are doing a very detailed drawing.

Seascapes are usually more interesting if there is subject matter in the foreground (even if it is only a few rocks or an extra-special wave). Painters of the old school often put in a red marker buoy to add interest to the foreground.

If you are trying to do waves in pencil you are tempting providence; it is sufficient to get the *feel* of waves, and not be precise. Waves are good for painting, but not for pencil work, and seascapes in pencil can never be really convincing. They should be regarded as sketches for paintings. Seascapes are among the most enjoyable type of pictures to do.

It is very restful to look at the sea, and if you have a seascape in mind remember how waves react, how they form and break, and how, very important, they fit into a pattern of other waves and water movement. The *look* of the sea is far more significant than the accuracy of the odd wave. Nowhere is reference to photographs of other artists' work so useful as in depicting the sea; everyone has their own method. The Venetians such as Canaletto used an unconvincing pattern of flat U-shapes, but others have done really convincing seas, even quite minor artists now almost forgotten.

Photographs of seas are useful but not as much as photographs of other artists' endeavours, who somehow had to express the constantly moving. Television and video are enormous helps in letting us see, via the freeze frame in video, exactly what water in motion looks like.

Waves, too, obey the laws of perspective, and recede according to the rules; they also have shadows, often forgotten to judge by the blobs of blue and green in the paintings of real novices.

PICTURE MAKING

It is easy to get preoccupied with the various kinds of paints, watercolours, oils, acrylic, pastels and other materials and think they are divided into exclusive compartments. They do require different equipment, but if divisions are to be made there are just two – paints which go with water and paints which go with oils. However even this div-

ision is not sacred. For example, the sculptor Henry Moore uses oil pastels and watercolours for his drawings, which do not mix. That is why he uses them. His aim is to make the oil-pastel drawing stand out from the background, so he uses the oil pastel first for his main features and then covers the paper with a watercolour wash, which, being repelled by the oil pastels, fills in the area not covered by the initial drawing. The work done in pastel therefore comes through boldly.

So when you start off a picture, do not have too definite a view of the end product. If it is a drawing it might be advantageous to develop it into a watercolour or a pastel, or if it is a watercolour it can turn into an acrylic or if you size over the watercolour into an oil painting. Similarly a drawing in oil pastel can turn into an oil painting. If this seems about to happen, you do not always need to size the paper, but let the oil paint soak into the surface. This results in a flat matt rather intriguing surface.

When you are working outdoors you have to be careful about how much equipment to take with you, but indoors there is a lot to be said for having *all* your painting equipment within easy reach. This can be a glorious muddle, and if you have a large table or working surface so much the better.

In picture making you have a number of choices. You can use pencil sketches made beforehand, or you can build up the painting as you go along, leaving some of it to chance. The 'blob' school of watercolour painters who included many good English watercolourists of the turn of the century laid down small splashes of colour and then meditated upon them until they could see an embryo picture – rather like looking at pictures in the fire. In some of his watercolour work J. M. W. Turner did much the same.

If you use preliminary sketches you can either reproduce them more or less exactly, or you can shift the subject around to make the picture hang together better – in other words making a composition of it. But there are certain subjects you may want to set down accurately. If you are doing

A typically adventurous painting by Turner in which the oil paint is used in a watercolourish manner, allowing the canvas to show through. This painting gives the impression of having been formed from accidental blotches and blobs of paint, though Turner was the last man to reveal the secrets of his techniques.

a painting of your house you do not want to shift around the chimneys, alter the disposition of the rose bushes in the garden, or change the shapes of tree branches to make them look more artistic. You want a record, just as you do if you undertake a portrait. Similarly if you are doing a well-loved landscape, you do not want to move around the elements to make it pretty. You want it as it is, warts and all.

Remember that you are doing the picture for yourself. A visual autobiography can be enchanting to look back on, charting not only past events but your increase in expertise. If this is the reason you paint, nurture it – and *do not throw anything away!* Even if the picture does not quite come off, it may bring back memories. No one is going to give you a prize for a better-than-average picture.

If the picture you are doing is imaginary, even if based on a real subject, you can include anything in it, including the improbable and impossible. Fantasy pictures are immense fun to do

and may have some therapeutic benefit. If you know the rules, it is sometimes refreshing to forget them, and have different perspectives in the same picture, or even eliminate perspective altogether. Or even make up your own, the practice of the contemporary primitive British artists currently enjoying a vogue.

Reference has already been made to composition. This is something you can take into account or discard. At its simplest, composition is making an interesting picture from a boring subject, and there is a good analogy in photography. Every photographic album contains architectural views – Salisbury Cathedral, Shakespeare's birthplace, or Stonehenge. How utterly boring most of these photographs are, the building set in the middle of the snap, nothing in the foreground except grass or a loved one. When we look at a professional's photograph of the same subject, what a difference! The professional looks at angles, the light, foreground interest (and is concerned with keeping

Salisbury Cathedral from the Meadows by John Constable. Places of architectural interest have long been a favourite subject for painters.

Two lively high-toned illustrations. Mediterranean scenes of this nature benefit from a fluid technique with the colour applied loosely.

the camera still).

When you are sketching or painting on the spot it is sometimes difficult to decide which is the best vantage point (and sometimes you will not be able to get at the best vantage point because there is already something there such as an intrusive building). If you do not particularly want an exact visual record, then you can alter things when you get home.

The most important point about composition is to get the spectator to look *into* the picture and not *across* it, to focus on an area of interest, not necessarily in the centre. Degas often had his focal point at the extreme edge of the picture. If you can get the eye to come to rest on something in the picture so much the better. The most obvious way is to use perspective, the receding lines leading into the focal point, and in some way blocking them so that they do not lead out again. You can improve composition by raising or lowering the horizon, and

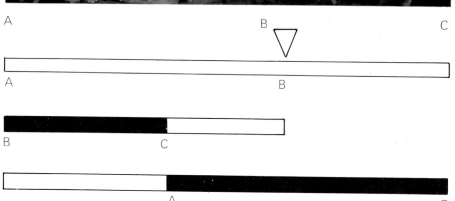

you can use shadows to direct the attention. Foreground detail can also draw the viewer in, and if overloaded can keep the attention there. Though it may be that this is what you want.

In the old days there were reckoned to be golden rules of composition, and much time was spent by theorists in analysing the works of the great masters of the Renaissance to see how they behaved or how they fell short. To some of these self-styled experts, painting was geometry in action, and joy was unconfined when they found this or that painter using the rules, especially when the subject of a well-known picture was in the form of a triangle (in Virgin and Child pictures it would have been difficult to avoid). Even better when one triangle on its base was balanced by an inverted triangle, or there were intricate interrelated triangles to glorify.

It is probable that artists such as the 15th-century Italian artist Piero della Francesca used a geometrical scaffold to base pictures on, and many artists, such as Hogarth, have published their ideas, though Hogarth does not seem to have acted on his theory of the 'curve of beauty'. There is therefore a lot of weighty theory about classical composition, and it can be satisfying to sketch in a geometrical figure and use it as the basis of a picture. But what is good composition to one can be boring to another. If composition can render a service, it is to stop the subject matter 'leaking' out of the edge of the picture.

One of the questions that arises if you are doing a watercolour (but not an oil) is whether to put in the outer limits of the picture when you start, in other words rule in a border. With a canvas you naturally cover the whole area. There are no hard and fast rules about a border; it helps some, hinders others, but if you are keen on composition and a balanced scheme then a border can be an asset. If you paint in a fantasy or formal style a decorated border can be an advantage – if it is carried out systematically. A geometric border which gets tedious because of the repetition and is skimped is worse than nothing at all. If the edges of a watercolour are getting ragged and inconclusive remember that you can always hide them under a mount – or cut them off.

If you are embarking on a fantasy or surrealist picture in the style of Dali or Chirico, try and keep to the same technique throughout. You can mix your mediums, but a medley of styles in the same picture never really works. It can be great fun working in someone else's style, doing a pastiche.

You must not feel you are being curtailed, and that certain techniques are artistically out of bounds. Not everyone has the egotism of certain famous painters who feel that even their thumb print is of value to someone. There are still numbers of techniques waiting to be found: so far as I know, nobody has yet experimented with painting on polystyrene ceiling tiles.

If you are one of those people who sets out on a project with a set idea and are reluctant to be diverted from your path, you may think it trivial to doodle, or let the painting take over. A bit of

In both of these compositions, by Turner (above) and L. S. Lowry (below), the selection of ingredients appears to be random. In fact, the focal points – the black mill in the case of Lowry, and the animal in Turner – are placed along the line of the Golden Section.

Left, above: A renaissance painting using three inter-linked triangles as the basis of its composition.

Left, centre: An English painting using the con-structional basis of two .interlinked triangles.

Left, below: A diagram illustrating the 'Golden Section', the ideal ratios, used by many classical artists as an aid to com-position. It is the division of a line in which the smaller part is in the same ratio to the greater part as the greater part is to the whole.

doodling, if you happen to be a name, can be worth a quarter of a million pounds.

On 23 March 1983 there was a sale of modern and Impressionist art at Sotheby's, London. One of the pictures on show was *Nocturne* by the Spanish painter Joan Miro. The estimate was £150,000–£200,000, and in the event it made £270,000. This is how Miro himself – a charming artist with a rich vein of invention – described the origin of the painting, in 1940–41:

'After my work (on oil paintings) I dipped my brushes in petrol and wiped them on the white sheets of paper from the album with no preconceived ideas. The blotchy surface put me in a good mood and provoked the birth of forms, human figures, animals, stars, the sky, and the moon and the sun. . . . Once I had managed to obtain a plastic equilibrium and bring order among all these elements, I began to paint in gouache, with the minute detail of a craftsman and a primitive.'

A painting by Miro, one of whose paintings realized £270,000 in March 1983.

Colour Schemes

Each painter has favourite colours and combinations of colours, and sometimes these are so personal to the artist that you can pick out the painter not by his style or subject matter but by the general colour scheme. Tubes of paint, especially oils but not acrylics, are marked with their degree of permanence, usually by a series of asterisks. The more asterisks, the more permanent. You may or may not take any notice of these asterisks; they are not important, and what are known as 'fugitive colours' will last as long as most of us want them to. I used so-called fugitive colours because I liked them 30 years ago, and they have not altered one iota from that day to this. So do not hesitate to use the 'fancy' colours such as Antwerp blue, Hooker's green, and Naples yellow; Naples yellow is a delightful colour, halfway between ordinary yellow and yellow ochre and many artists would not be without it as a multi-purpose colour. More important is that cer-

tain colours are 'loose' and have a limited covering capacity. Sap green, one of the 'fancy' colours, is useful but lacks bite.

A traditional watercolour palette that has much to commend it is the following: *Chrome lemon; Yellow ochre; Alizarin crimson; Light red; Vermilion; Prussian blue; Cobalt blue; Ultramarine; Raw sienna; Burnt sienna; Vandyke brown; Viridian; Ivory black.*

Many artists used a very limited range of colours. Jean Millet (1814–1875), whose painting *The Angelus* was once one of the half-dozen most famous paintings in the world, often used a palette of no more than five colours: *Iron oxide red* or *Vermilion*; a *Brown earth colour* of the Burnt sienna variety; a *Blue/Green*; a *Black*; and *White*.

A modern artist who imposed a similar restraint on his palette was L. S. Lowry. In his own words: 'I am a simple man, and I use simple materials: *Ivory black; Vermilion; Prussian blue; Yellow ochre; Flake white* – and no medium. That's all I've ever used for my painting.'

The writer on art A. W. Rich advises a palette of five colours: *Light red; Yellow ochre; Cyanine blue; Ivory black; Burnt sienna.* As a concession, the same authority allows five more colours: *Viridian; Raw sienna; Ultramarine; Aureolin; Rose madder.* The great drawback of this palette is that it lacks a vivid red.

Many of the great artists of the past used a very extensive range of colours, though Titian maintained that a painter needed only three colours. Nevertheless, he used nine colours: *Lead white; Ultramarine; Madder lake; Burnt sienna; Malachite green; Yellow ochre; Red ochre; Orpiment* (literally translated as 'gold paint'); *Ivory black.*

Van Eyck had a palette of eight colours: *Brown; Madder; Ultramarine; Yellow ochre; Terre verte* (a green); *Orpiment; Red ochre; Peach black.*

Rubens used a large number of colours: *Lead white; Orpiment; Yellow ochre; Yellow lake; Madder; Vermilion; Red ochre; Ultramarine; Cobalt blue; Terre verte; Malachite green; Burnt sienna; Ivory black.*

The writer on art Hilaire Hiler, whose *The Painter's Pocket Book* (1937) is the best book of its kind ever written, gives a choice of two palettes, one low-toned, the other high-toned. The low one was: *Titanium white; Yellow ochre; Light red; Cobalt blue; Ultramarine.* The high-toned one was: *Titanium white; Cadmium yellow; Ultramarine; Cadmium red; Lamp black.*

In 1876 the aesthete P. G. Hamerton (1834–1894) declared what he thought was a basic essential palette. Hamerton was an artist of a kind, but is best-known as a moderately influential critic of the middle-of-the-road school. These are the colours a good Victorian would have used: *Flake white; Pale Cadmium yellow; Vermilion; Rose madder; Ultramarine; Emerald green; Vandyke brown; Black.*

It is interesting to compare this palette with that of the great Impressionist artist Renoir (1841–1919) at the same time: *Flake white; Naples yellow; Chrome yellow; Cobalt* or *Ultramarine; Alizarin*

red; *Viridian; Emerald green; Vermilion.* Notice that Renoir did not use blacks at this time.

Renoir's palette was not so different from that of Georges Seurat (1859–1891), who evolved the 'pointillist' technique, in which separate dots of primary colours such as blue and yellow were placed side by side and intended to be interpreted by the human eye as green: *White;* an *Orange; Raw sienna; Alizarin red; Ultramarine; Cobalt blue* and perhaps *Cerulean blue; Vermilion; Emerald green; Viridian; Cadmium yellow; Yellow ochre.*

Vincent van Gogh also eschewed the use of black: *Lead white; Red lake; Vermilion; Cadmium yellow; Ultramarine; Cobalt blue; Cobalt violet; Emerald green; Viridian;* an earth colour probably *Sienna,* burnt or raw.

A palette suitable for acrylic painting could be

A painting by Lowry showing the self-imposed limited palette.

A group of apples by Cézanne, well illustrating the painter's brush work.

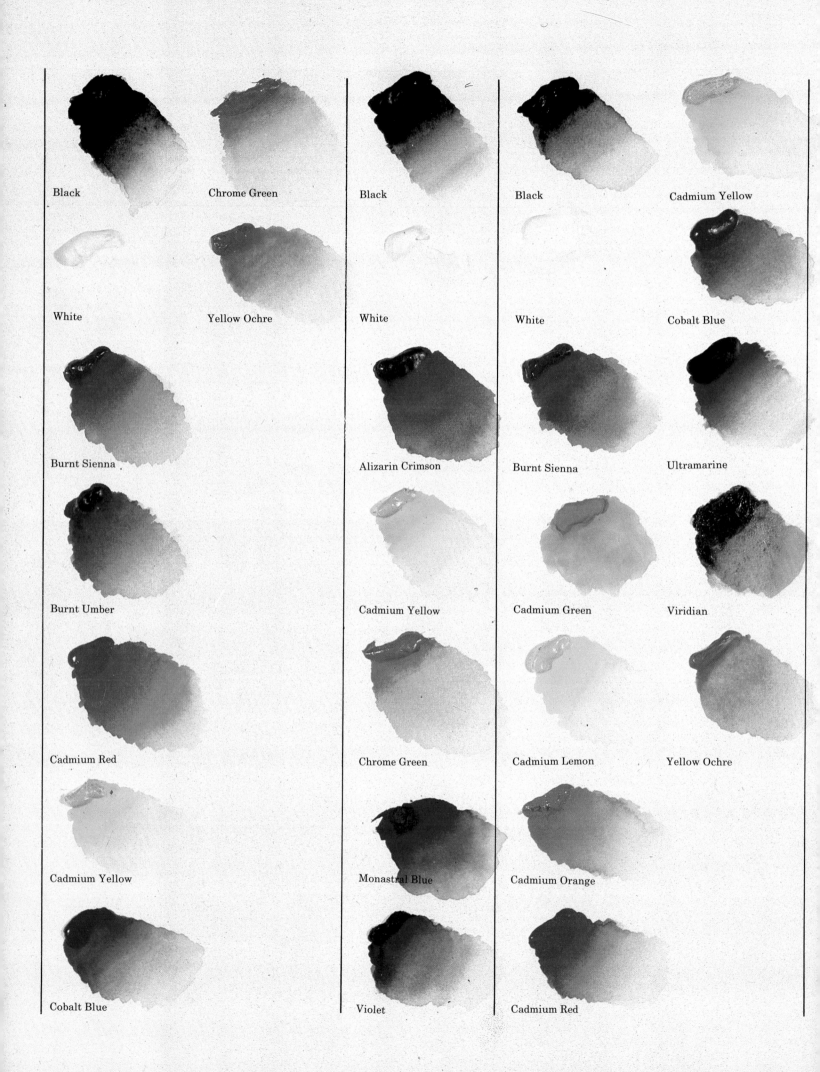

Black

Chrome Green

Black

Black

Cadmium Yellow

White

Yellow Ochre

White

White

Cobalt Blue

Burnt Sienna

Alizarin Crimson

Burnt Sienna

Ultramarine

Burnt Umber

Cadmium Yellow

Cadmium Green

Viridian

Cadmium Red

Chrome Green

Cadmium Lemon

Yellow Ochre

Cadmium Yellow

Monastral Blue

Cadmium Orange

Cobalt Blue

Violet

Cadmium Red

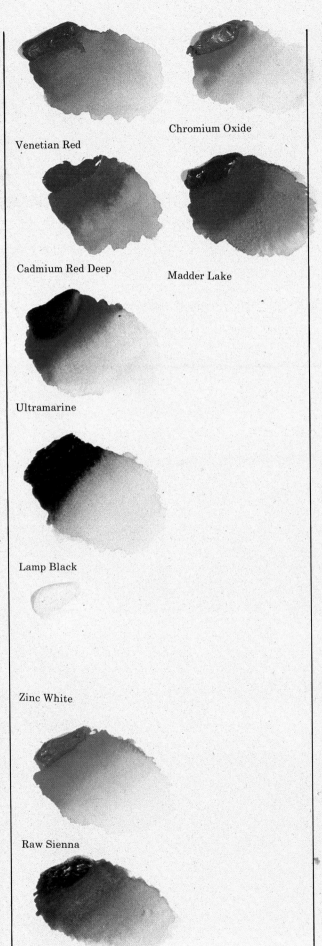

Venetian Red

Chromium Oxide

Cadmium Red Deep

Madder Lake

Ultramarine

Lamp Black

Zinc White

Raw Sienna

Burnt Umber

made up of the following: a *Green*; *Burnt* and *Raw umber*; *Cadmium yellow*; *Cadmium red*; *Crimson*; *Raw sienna*; *Ultramarine*; *Cobalt blue*; *Black*; *White*.

Suggesting a range of pastel colours is more difficult as there are so many – several hundred – to choose from, many of them greys, blue-greys, red-greys and several kinds of white. The colours vary between different manufacturers, and initially it is probably best to rely on boxed sets. Some of the makers provide separate sets for landscape and portrait work, but if you wish to start off by buying individual sticks use one of the ranges recommended for paints and add a few assorted greys.

Most of the palettes listed are general purpose ranges, but if you have in mind a green-based colour scheme you could restrict your choice to: *Black*; *White*; *Burnt sienna*; *Burnt umber*; *Cadmium red*; *Cadmium yellow*; *Cobalt blue*; *Chrome green*; *Yellow ochre*. Red mixed into a green is an admirable 'cooling down' colour. The chief fault of novice landscapists is to make the greens far too green and brash.

A rather cold colour scheme is: *Black*; *White*; *Alizarin crimson*; *Cadmium yellow*; *Chrome green*; *Monastral blue*; *Violet*.

A hot somewhat acid scheme is: *Black*; *White*; *Burnt sienna*: *Cadmium green*; *Cadmium lemon*; *Cadmium orange*; *Cadmium red*; *Cadmium yellow*; *Cobalt blue*; *Ultramarine*; *Viridian*; *Yellow ochre*.

An interesting palette evolved by a pre-war chemist named Toch guaranteed permanency of pigments: *Venetian* or *Light red*; *Medium cadmium*; *Ultramarine*; *Lamp black*; *Zinc white*; *Raw sienna*; *Burnt umber*; *Chromium oxide* (yellow); *Madder lake*.

These selections are only a handful of the hundreds of different schemes used by artists, and everyone will want to create their own. Some of the pigments used by the great painters of the past are not available at art-shops, perhaps fortunately for many of the masterpieces we take so much for granted have been repainted so many times that they can hardly be called original works of art, since they have been repainted because the colour has literally disappeared or been transmuted. In Antwerp Museum there is a trunk containing the powdered colours used by Rubens (putting colour into tubes is fairly recent, dating back to the 1840s). The ultramarine, the madders, the lead white and all those browny colours known as earth colours have survived well, but the yellow lake, the vegetable greens and vermilion have almost entirely faded away. The ultramarine of the old painters was originally made from lapis lazuli, but even before the Second World War this was more than a pound sterling a tiny pan and is now virtually priceless. The modern equivalent is French ultramarine, the principal ingredients of which are sulphur and sodium.

Scientists have discovered (or decided) that there are 80,000 tints between white and black. Within a range of 20 colours or so most of us can get what we want.

An evocative photograph giving some idea of the materials available to painters of the past, and the problems posed by them – nothing in tubes and the need to mix the pigments with mortar and pestle.

CHAPTER 2

OILS

WHAT ARE OIL PAINTS?

Most pigments are multi-purpose; oil paints are pigments blended with oil. They are put on a surface with a brush or a palette knife, either neat from the tube or mixed with something to make the paint run nicely. There is always learned dispute as to which is more difficult, oils or watercolours, and there is no answer. Neither is very difficult if you do not panic. Mistakes are easier to take out in oils, and you can use a canvas over and over again.

WHAT MATERIALS ARE NEEDED?

Paints These come in tubes, and there is an immense range. So-called 'students' colours are now labelled differently, and are much cheaper than 'artists' colours. Buying expensive ranges offers no real advantage as most paints will outlast you and your children. Until the last century artists made their own pigments from powdered colours, and as this was often a hit-or-miss system, especially when the artist was drunk, some of these hand-made colours were so fugitive that they could disappear from the canvas within a few years. Buy big tubes rather than little tubes; if you take the trouble to keep the top on, the paint will stay moist for years and years. I use paints which I bought in the 1950s and they are as good as new. Tubes are always well labelled, and these labels are marked with asterisks to indicate the degree of permanence. This is not very important. To all intents and purposes the colours will stay the same.

Mediums and Glosses There are many of these but the most popular is turpentine, which imparts a matt finish and is very good for detailed work. Most other mediums give a slight gloss, and some of those put out by the large manufacturers include varnish as well as linseed oil. These ready-made mediums are very good, and really there is no need to look further. Poppy oil is a slow-drying medium, liquin is a fast dryer. Some painters do not use medium at all, but use the paint straight from the tube. Others use varnish. If you are sensitive to the smell of turpentine, use white spirit, and ironmongers' turpentine is much cheaper and just as good as the turpentine sold in art shops.

Varnish There is no need to use varnish at all, though you will find that if you use a medium other than turpentine the degree of gloss finish will be variable, and you will want to use a varnish to give an even appearance to the picture surface. Varnishes can be glossy or matt, and a retouching varnish is useful for areas that unaccountably have gone flat. Two coats of thin varnish are better than one coat of thick, and you do not have to wait too long for coats to dry. Some people do not advise varnishing a picture until it has been painted for weeks or months, but you will find that you can do this job as soon as the paint is dry. The thicker the paint layer (or 'impasto') the slower it is to dry, and white is one of the slower dryers, probably because it is applied more thickly for highlights. Many artists find that a flat square-edged soft brush is the best to apply varnish; if you use a bristle, there is a chance of the varnish getting a scratchy look when it dries out.

Brushes Some people prefer a lot of brushes, some a few, and many have their favourite brushes which they have broken in and would not drop for the world. You can use hard brushes or soft brushes; even if you are working on a large scale you can use soft brushes throughout. You have a choice of natural bristle or hair, and nylon, which comes in soft and hard grades and lasts longer than natural products. Artists who work on a small scale or who are keen on detail use small soft brushes; however if you are using sable you can get through two or three (or more) brushes in the course of one picture. After painting, clean your brushes by taking off the surplus paint with tissues or rags and rinsing them in turpentine or white spirit. Every so often, say once a month, wash the brushes using household soap and hot water, drawing the brush handle first through the soap surface and then rinsing under a hot tap. Despite the best care, paint brushes can get clogged, and a commercial brush cleaner such as Polyclens can come in handy. Paint always clogs at the end of the ferrule, and after a time it becomes hard, even if you religiously clean your brushes. Sometimes a proprietary cleaner is necessary. Brushes should be kept upright in a pot, handles down, with perhaps something like a jam jar to put the smaller sable or nylon brushes in so that they do not rub against the side of a larger pot.

A basic brush kit consists of: a small, medium and large round bristle; a small, medium and large flat bristle; a small, medium and large round sable (or nylon); a small, medium and large flat sable (or nylon); an ordinary household painting brush to put on a priming coat to a canvas or board; and, an added option, a 'fan' brush, in which the hairs come out in the form of a fan, useful for blending. An old shaving brush can also come in handy for giving textures.

Palette Knives These come in various sizes, and a small, medium and large should be bought. They are used to clean paint from a palette, or to apply paint to a canvas. You can use palette knives to paint an entire picture, or you can merely use them to deposit the paint on the canvas and then employ brushes. Some artists prefer to keep a layer of old paint on the palette knife, others prefer them pristine. The metal of the smaller knives is very thin, and if encrusted paint needs to be removed do it gently as the blades are easily damaged. Always store your knives in a safe place, as otherwise the blades may be accidentally bent.

Newcomers should not feel they are bound to paint in a certain circumscribed manner, and a fresh attitude towards unusual subjects, as here, can result in a striking and novel picture.

Detail of one of the heads in the above picture, treated in the way in which Cézanne portrayed apples.

A selection of palette knives of various shapes and sizes.

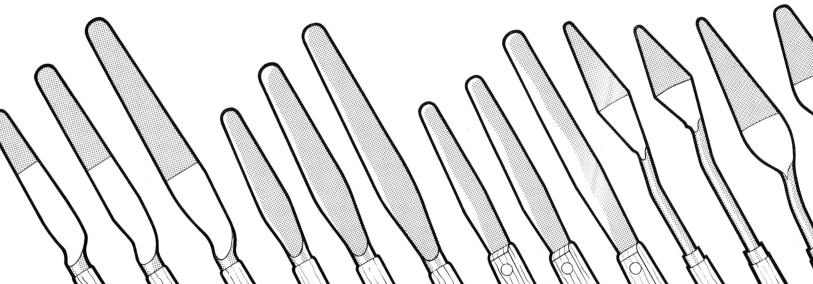

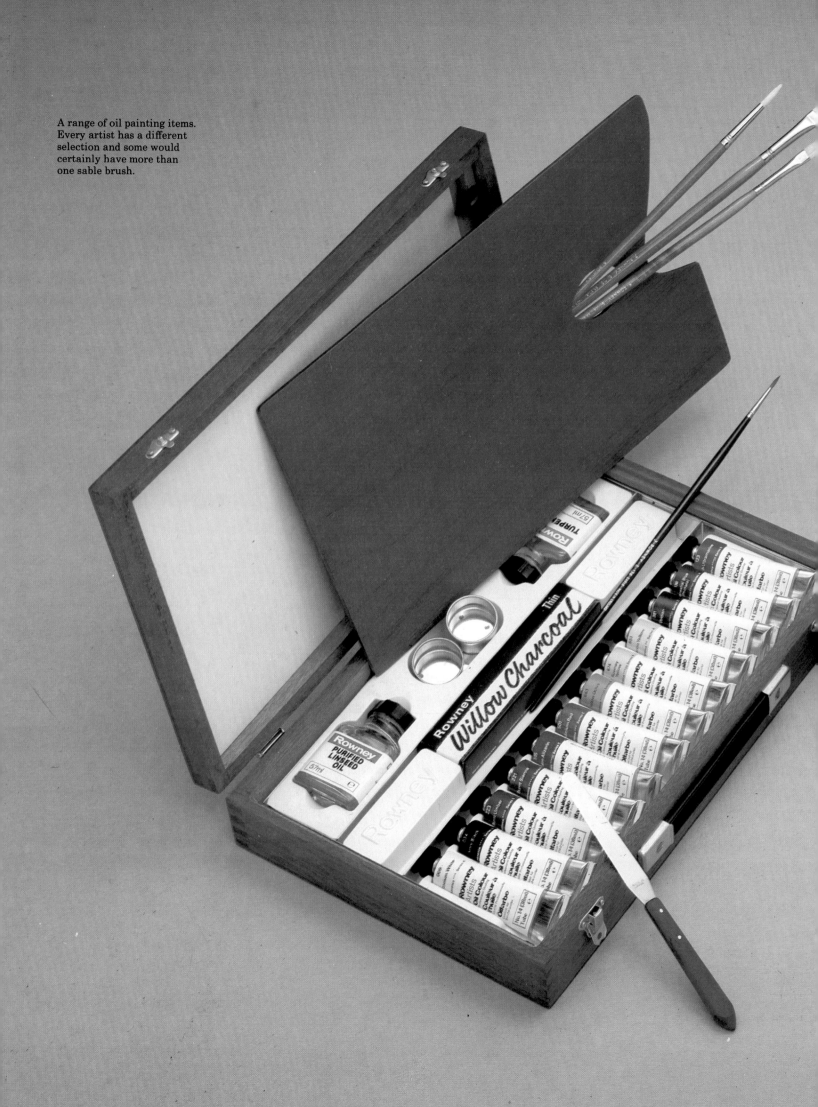

A range of oil painting items.
Every artist has a different
selection and some would
certainly have more than
one sable brush.

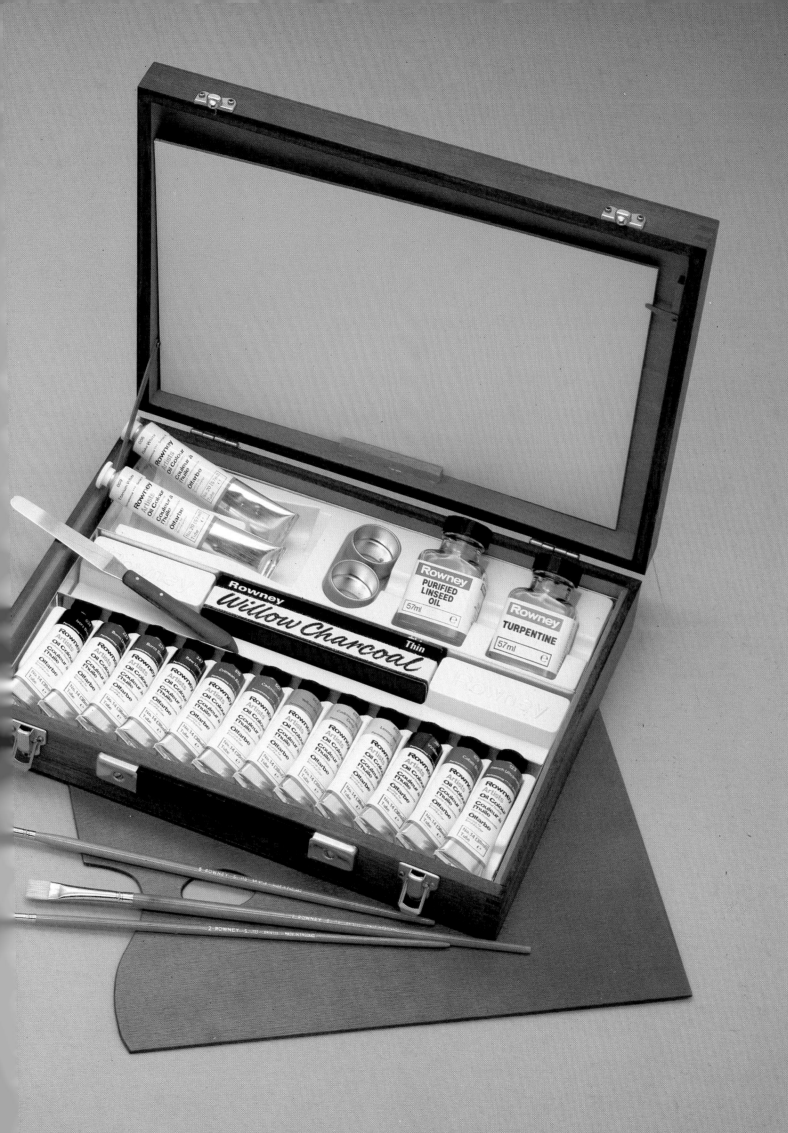

An artist in his studio.
Notice the large professional
easel and the canvas at
comfortable eye level.

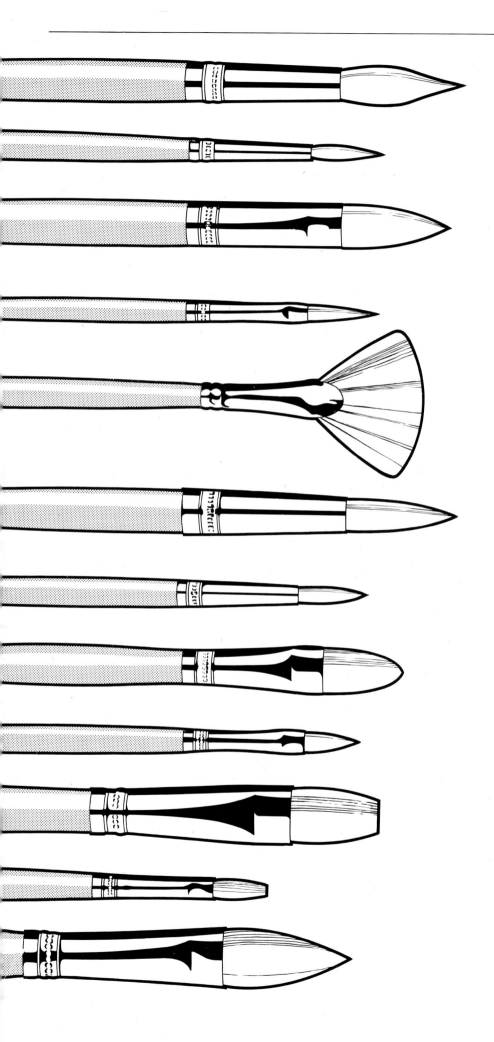

A selection of brushes. Some you will find more useful than others, but don't be afraid to experiment, using both bristle and hair brushes for oil painting, and not forgetting nylon.

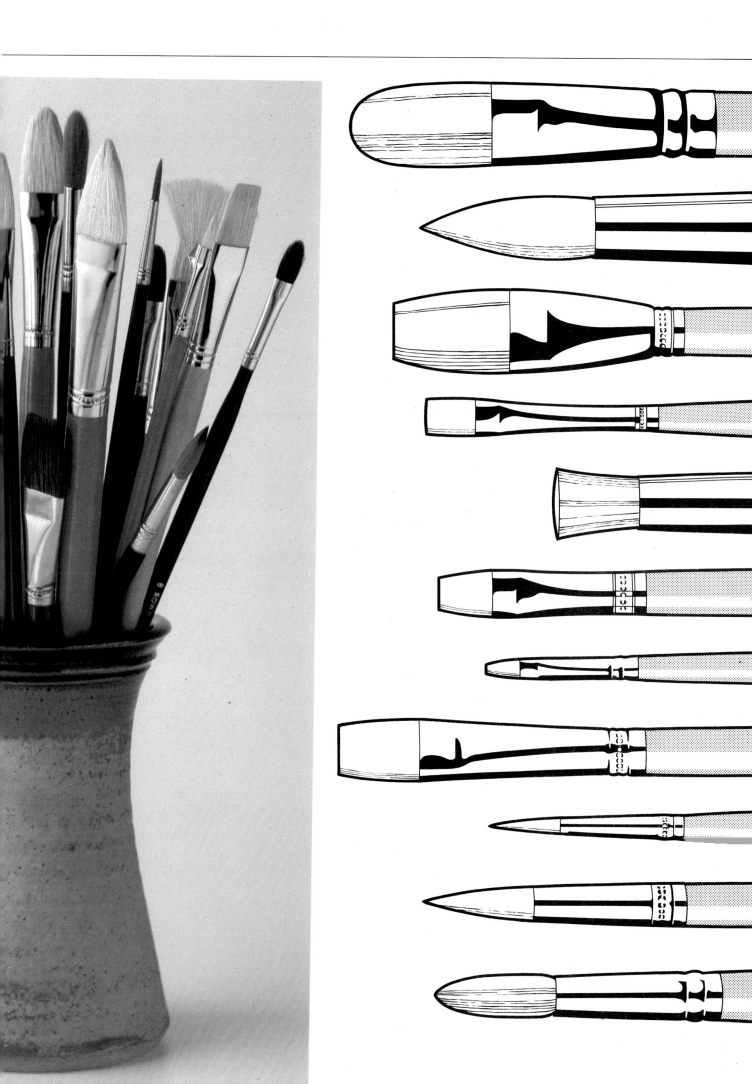

Palettes Palettes were once made of wood, probably for no better reason than that colours were basically muted and earthy, and wood seemed an appropriate surface. Palettes have a hole in them through which the thumb fits, and now come in plastic, tin, china, aluminium, wood and paper (throwaway palettes). You may not want to use a palette at all, finding it a nuisance, in which case a large plate is just as good. If you are sitting down to do your picture, it is better, as the dished sides prevent the paint from slopping over the top. If you are using a traditional palette, you can get small metal containers which fix to the side of the palette and contain your turpentine or other medium. If you are using a dinner plate, the tops of jars can serve as containers, and be thrown away when the medium begins to coagulate or get dirty. Plastic and tin palettes have circular depressions in them for the paint, but these are often more annoying than useful. If you wish to mix your paints thoroughly, cake-tins are far more convenient.

Canvases The traditional surface for oil paint is canvas, but although the 'give' of canvas, which is on a stretcher and therefore has no backing, is pleasant, there are many cheaper substitutes for canvas, some of which cost nothing, and can be rescued from the attic, from under the stairs, or from the garage. One of the best surfaces to work on is ordinary cardboard, which merely needs sizing and maybe priming. There is also oil-painting board, oil-painting paper (sold in blocks like sketch-pads), wood panels, hardboard (rough or smooth side), and, indeed, almost anything. Oil-painting boards come in a variety of textures, from very smooth to rough. Plywood is a delightful surface to work on, and just needs a coat of size. Much depends on whether you like a rough tooth, or smooth, or no tooth at all. Generally speaking, if you are using stiff brushes you will need a surface with a tooth.

Easel Even if you prefer to work at a table with the canvas or board horizontal, an easel is very handy, if only as somewhere to prop up a picture to see how it is progressing. If you are working broadly or on a large scale, an easel is essential – or at least an easel-type object. A child's blackboard makes a substitute. Professional artists' easels can be huge contraptions, and a smaller travelling easel will serve most of us well enough.

Drawing Board If you use traditional canvases or canvas board you may not need a drawing board, but if you use oil-painting paper you will. Oil-painting paper is sold in sheets or in a block, but although the block has a thick cardboard backing it is often more convenient to take off each sheet as it is needed. When fixing oil-painting paper or anything which needs to be pinned to the drawing board, put a pad of newspaper over the drawing board, covering it. This provides a perfect working surface, and also the newspaper is very handy to try your paint on, to see if you have the right colour, and also to get rid of any surplus medium on your brush. If you work fast and want to get the colours on right away, this is much more convenient than looking around for a piece of paper.

As you get into oil painting there are extra bits and pieces which you will want to add to your basic equipment, and many of these you will discover for yourself. A piece of *sponge* is one of these accessories. You may wonder why, as sponges naturally go with water, and oil clogs them. Sponges have as a matter of fact been used in painting for some considerable time, to give texture to paint already applied with a brush, and as a painting instrument. We have all seen those ready-made Victorian landscapes with a lake, trees, a bright blue sky, and a yacht in the water. The trees seem to be spattered in, with tiny globules of pigment; the leaves were put in with a piece of sponge, and although flashy these trees can look very effective from a distance. These pictures, now in such demand by interior decorators, were hack work for the lower end of the market, and were turned out in less than half an hour to a simple formula. For newcomers to oil painting who want to get an easy effect – and no harm in that – a good look at some of these pictures can be helpful. The Victorian painters used natural sponges, because there were no synthetic substitutes, but household and car sponges, at a fraction of the cost, serve almost as well if the sharp corners are cut off with a pair of scissors so that you have an irregularly shaped object. If you want

to do sponge painting on a fairly small scale, cut off a little portion of sponge and hold it in a Bulldog clip for easy handling.

Another unlikely accessory is *tissue paper*, not household tissues which have a dimpled appearance, but ordinary tissue paper as used to wrap up articles in shops. This is to remove the surplus oil and paint off a painting while it is still wet, and it is a trick much employed by British painters of the earlier part of this century. It adds subtlety and atmosphere, and is placed over the moist painting, and gently pressed, being taken up when you think that it has absorbed sufficient paint. It is known as 'tonking' after Professor Tonks, a teacher at the Slade School, who pioneered this extremely effective dodge. If you feel that your colouring is too strong and you have not succeeded in getting the picture to hang together, tonking is recommended – and if you find you do not like the effect you can always put the paint back on with a brush.

Sometimes you need a starting-off point for a painting. A few ambiguous dabs of a paint-soaked sponge can do this on the pictures-in-a-fire principle, but tissue paper from a successfully tonked picture can also do this, leaving enigmatic traces of paint on the new surface, ready to spark off the imagination. A surprising number of painters in the past, including Turner, have used random touches of paint to help them on their way, and oil paints, with their richness and variety, are ideal for adventure and experiment. If it fails, all you do is to get a cloth soaked in turpentine and wipe it

A painting and details of it,
showing a 'fruity' style with
plenty of paint generously
applied.

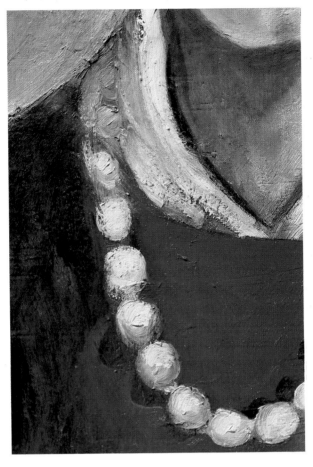

all off. It is a method well worth trying.

There is no doubt about it, oil paints can be very messy, and a painter's smock is not a quaint garment but very functional. Paint has a habit of dripping down the brush and getting on to the hands, and thus on to clothes, and it is always a good idea to be well provided with household tissues and lots of rag, to clean up the handles of brushes, to wipe surplus paint from the business end of brushes, to clear unwanted areas of paint off a canvas, and to wipe a palette clean when you feel that it has got altogether too congested.

Other items you may need are dividers, to get distances right between various sections of the picture, and a *mahl stick*. This is a wooden rod, often in three telescopic sections fitted together with brass ferules, with a rounded tip. This is to rest the hand on while you are doing fine detailed work, the rounded end on the canvas or support, the right hand holding the brush resting on the stick itself, and the left hand holding the far end. An ordinary length of garden cane is a decent substitute for a mahl stick. As in other mediums, cotton buds come in very handy, removing surplus paint off a canvas, tidying up areas, or distributing paint more evenly on the canvas. It is sometimes easier to do this with a cotton bud than a brush.

In addition there are the various items needed when setting down the outlines of an oil painting. Almost anything has been used for this purpose, with the favourite possibly charcoal. Pencils, pens, felt pens, ball-point pens, pastel, all can be pressed into service.

There is one piece of equipment which you will have to make yourself (if there is one on the market few have seen it). This is an aid to help you draw a straight line. The answer is to get a straight edge, preferably wood, and nail or glue together two blocks of wood on it, one at each end, far enough apart to reach dry canvas or, if using oil-painting paper, the drawing board. These blocks should not be more than half an inch high; if they are, the brush will be difficult to control, and if the blocks are not high enough the hairs of the brush will rub against the straight edge, thus damaging them. This do-it-yourself instrument can be very useful, not only in oil painting, but in acrylics and water-colour. Drawing a straight line freehand is *not* easy, and almost on the level of difficulty of drawing a perfect circle. If you are doing sea pictures and the ropes and tackle need to be taut and straight, this ruler-on-stilts can be indispensable.

HOW DO I START?

With some mediums such as pastels and water-colours you can take them up as and when it suits you, for as short a time as you want, but if you are going to paint in oils you do need a little preparation in order to avoid getting in a mess. If you are working on the flat, use pads of newspapers to cover the surfaces. These not only absorb blobs of paint or splashes of turpentine, but prevent them from going on to sensitive surfaces. Go through your brushes and check them to see that they are reasonably clean, and pick out the ones you are likely to use. Squeeze out the colours on your palette. Some artists have a set order, light to dark (white, yellow, orange, blue, green, brown, black), but others put them down in any order. If you like a specific range of colours (see the chapter on colour schemes) you will no doubt get into the habit of placing the colours in some kind of order, but many painters put out the colours they feel they want to use in this particular picture.

There is no need to clean the palette after each painting session. When there is old paint on the palette, often in a mix, it can be used to evolve new colour blends. It is a question of personality. Some artists like to start with a pristine palette, and traces of previous paint are a personal affront. If you are of this temperament it is worth while using paper throwaway palettes. Sometimes there comes a time when even the most reluctant palette-cleaner finds that the palette is completely clogged up. In this case, get a strong paint stripper such as Nitromors and clear the old paint completely. Although oil paint takes a considerable time to dry out, it will acquire a thin shell after three or four days. This can be taken off using the tip of a palette knife.

Mediums, especially the ready-made ones with an element of varnish, also film over after a time, and this crust can again be picked off with a palette knife. Turpentine evaporates, but at no great rate, but it is advisable to keep it in a jar with a screw-on lid. But do not be niggardly about turpentine; it is cheap, and if you are covering a large area you will find it convenient to use it from a small bowl, preferably a pottery and not plastic one. Some plastics melt when exposed to strong liquids.

If you are using an easel, make certain that it is at a convenient height and angle, and that the legs will not splay out as soon as you apply pressure to the canvas or working surface. If you prefer, sit down to the easel. Wind-up office chairs are better than ordinary dining or kitchen chairs, and a chair with arms can be infuriating. Make certain there is newspaper on the floor, or at least something which can be kept clean, and not carpet.

Keep the equipment you need within easy reach, and always have plenty of rags and tissues at hand. When you are setting up remember that if you are using natural light, and do not have a north window (where the light is constant), this will change in the course of a painting session.

'I have my equipment ready, and am working flat on a table. I have some smooth oil-painting paper. I have never touched a paint brush since I left school, I am by nature a meticulous sort of person, and I would like to do something simple and reasonably "like" and which does not look like something the dog trod in.'

One of the easiest kinds of picture to paint is a simple seascape. No complicated shadows are involved, and for the more ambitious there are extra

A step-by-step realization of a seascape; first the horizon, then the filling in of sea and sky and finally the last touches.

options to make the picture more interesting.

Place the board vertically, and two-thirds of the way down draw a straight line across, using measurements and a ruler. This is your skyline. This is the only preliminary work you will need to do. Mix a blue with white, not too much blue, plenty of white, and do not mix it too thoroughly, and add a splash of turpentine so that the colour runs nicely. Begin applying the paint with a medium bristle from the top down, darker blue at the top, near white at the bottom, where the skyline comes. *Option:* Go over this area with a medium soft brush, fusing in the blue and the white, and getting a more enamel-like surface. *Further Option:* Draw in clouds, using a little white maybe mixed with a trace of raw sienna or yellow ochre. If you wish have some shadow at the bottom of the clouds, use a very small amount of black or vandyke brown.

Mix a sea colour. Seas vary enormously, and you can select your own blend. Blue plus green is the traditional colour, but you can add browns and yellows. Paint the bottom third of the board with this mix, making certain that the paint at the top meets the sky perfectly horizontally. Use the side of a flat brush to make the meeting of the two colours clean. Make the bottom of the picture somewhat darker than the skyline area by adding a brown or a touch of black. *Option:* Go over this area with a medium soft brush. *Further Option:* Suggest waves by touches of white. Beneath the white add darker colours (blue plus brown, or green plus brown) to indicate shadow. If you have difficulty indicating waves in this way, look at photographs of pictures with waves in them.

Put in some land feature on the horizon. Burnt sienna with a touch of blue is suitable. This feature can be quite small, and as the sky is light you can overpaint. If the sky paint is too rich and not dry, take out the area you want to cover with a small palette knife, and then paint over. *Option:* Indicate some kind of shadow on the land, by either applying a touch of white, or a touch of darker colour.

Paint a ship somewhere in the middle of the sea area, not too far from the horizon (otherwise you are looking *down* on the ship which makes the shape less comprehensible). You are painting the shape of a ship, and you have the choice of two simple forms, a ship with a funnel or funnels, and a ship with sails. Do not be too ambitious. The ship merely serves as an accent. You may care to wait for the sea to dry, but otherwise with the point of a divider or similar pointed object such as the wrong end of a paint brush pick out in the wet paint the outline of your ship, removing the paint enclosed in your outline with a small palette knife. Then fill in, using black. *Option:* Add highlights on the ship using the smallest soft brush with white. Highlights can occur on the funnel, on the superstructure, or on the deck where the black meets the sea. On sails, the highlights can occur on one side or on the hull. *Further Option:* Add a trace of white where the bottom of the ship meets the waves. This white can be irregular, indicating the action of waves. Add birds at will (flat V-shapes in white against the sea, or black or grey against the sky).

Then you will have a simple picture. As such it will look neat and unpretentious. You can fill it in further if you wish, by adding foreground interest (a hemisphere in red, with the red darkened where it meets the sea – this is the traditional marine picture filler, a buoy). While the paint is still wet, you can modify the sky, by sunsetting it (a whisper of crimson in the blue/white), or adding a trace of yellow. You can make the clouds more specific. You can add a tiny ship on the horizon, using your smallest soft pointed brush, grading the colour down so that it is just visible against the sky. When the picture is dry, you can glaze it, putting on an overall coat of thin paint liberally diluted with either turpentine or medium. You can use almost any colour to transform the appearance of the picture, and you can apply further glazes as you wish. You can apply part glazes, covering one part of the picture. You may wish to darken the foreground with a glaze of dark brown or black. You may wish to brighten up an area of the sea with a glaze of white. When the glazes are dry, you can varnish if you wish (some pictures look better unvarnished and matt).

'I would like to try something a little more demanding, using traditional techniques.'

A landscape with hills in the background, a middle distance of trees, and a foreground of water. Mix your sky, blue and white, and keeping the top of the painting a darker tint apply the paint with a loaded bristle brush. If you have any sky colour left, add some red, and remix for the hills, laying in the colour with broad strokes, putting in your light and shade (darkening the mix with more blue or brown or lightening it with white or yellow). You can pick either side of the hills for your shadow area.

The trees in the middle distance are not too precise, yet not vague, and can be painted in either a mixed green (blue plus yellow) or a tube green such as chromium green with maybe a touch of Prussian blue. The bank on the far side of the water can be put in with yellow ochre with a dash of a green or blue. The water is put in with smooth horizontal strokes, blue, darkish green, with an added medium brown such as burnt sienna to cool the mix, and ripples added in white, using either the small bristle or the small soft brush. The reflections of the trees and the hills in the water are always vertically beneath the objects, similar colour but darker. You can break the outlines of the reflection by ripple.

The overall impression of the foreground can

When you have done the simple seascape it is no major step to a more adventurous composition, with a lighthouse as the major feature and giving more attention to the sea and sky without, however, being too precise.

A simple composition showing how to make a picture using the easiest of methods. Unadventurous perhaps, but certainly a picture.

Titanium White

Yellow Ochre

Burnt Umber

Cadmium Yellow

Viridian

Alizarin Crimson

French Ultramarine

These illustrations, and those on the following pages, demonstrate the progress of a simple still life from the original photograph to the finished painting, showing the intermediate steps.

Composition and eye level are very important when painting from still life. These sketches show some of the mistakes commonly made by beginners.

Objects are too formal.

The eye level is too low and the objects too central.

be thick and warm, using the bristle brush fully loaded with paint. You can either thoroughly blend your colours (green and red), or can apply them wet on wet individually, adding maybe yellow ochre. Dabbing the colour on gives the impression of rough ground, and by adding shadows in the foreground you can specify the nature of the ground (grass, stones, etc). You can add brown or black to your mix for shadow colour.

If the final picture seems tame, add further hills behind those already there in a lighter tone with more emphasis on the blue, or in the middle distance add a touch or two of pure colour, suggesting the presence of cottages or buildings, or even figures. You can refine the whole picture by making the focal point the far bank, picking out the trees with more detail, and adding fairly precise figures (remembering to include them in your reflections).

For more subtlety, blur the hill outlines with a flat brush, and then blur the foreground, so that only the middle distance is in any kind of focus. When you are blurring distances or foregrounds, it is better to do it in light horizontal sweeps, and remember to amend any clouds you may have put in.

In many pictures pure white clouds can freeze a picture, and yellow ochre and a hint of red mixed in with the white can provide a warmer less bracing touch. Clouds are always sharper in outline at the top than the bottom, and also lighter. The sky need not necessarily be blue; yellow, pink, and even purple can be used for dramatic effect. A glaring sun in the sky is difficult to pull off, but worth trying.

'I would like to do a simple still life in a rather different technique.'

Bottles and jugs, with the odd apple or orange, can be used almost at a moment's notice. Place a thin wash of colour over the canvas to establish a general tone, and then roughly draw in the objects in charcoal. Then take a flat soft brush, ½-inch or so, and using horizontal strokes *all the time* put in the shapes of the objects in their natural colour, or slightly subdued natural colour. Put in your background with rather thicker paint, not worrying if you are overlapping your objects, and then put in the darks of your principal items. You keep the same size brush throughout, though of course you can use two or three the same size if you wish to reserve one of the brushes for the lighter tones.

On top of the darks you put your half-tones, keeping the same *texture* of paint, and you can now use the brush vertically or diagonally, but keeping it flat and not overloading it with paint. Apply the highlights in white, still with the flat brush, but keep the whole composition muted. To increase the atmosphere you can gently add other colours – not necessarily those 'in life' but these additional colours are blended in to the basic colour. The whole surface of the painting will be regular, but avoid an egg-shell finish and allow the object edges to be a little fuzzy and indistinct.

This square brush technique was brought to

a peak of perfection by the Newlyn School of painters who flourished in Cornwall at the turn of the century and later, and it became a staple technique for art colleges throughout Britain. The practice of this method encourages sensitivity to tone. It is best practised with turpentine rather than with one of the juicier mediums, and pictures painted in this way do not need to be varnished. If you feel that the colours are too strident, you can 'tonk' the pictures, placing a sheet of tissue over the surface to absorb excess paint and moisture.

With oil paints there is no end to the possibilities and usable techniques, and it is the only medium where errors can be removed by the simple method of wiping them off with a cloth or scraping them off with a palette knife. If you wish to spend a fair amount of time on a painting use the methods employed by the great painters of the past (see chapter on Advanced Techniques). They painted in a series of transparent glazes, laying one on top of the other, building the picture up gradually. Another method is to carry out an underpainting in much diluted paint, staining rather than painting. The underpainting is not concerned with detail, but in establishing the areas of tone, and covering the white of the canvas. Whatever you are doing, it is often – even usually – better to tint the canvas. In an underpainting white is not used, the dark and light colours obtained by the amount of turpentine in the wash, and no more than four colours are needed – a blue, a couple of browns, and yellow ochre or raw sienna.

Once the tone of the picture has been set by the underpainting, the overpainting can be as thick as you like. It is often advisable to put the paint on in direct abrupt touches rather than stroking it on, without worrying too much about overlapping adjacent areas. Surplus paint can be scraped off or overpainted. But do not imagine that you have to be rough and ready to make a 'real' oil painting. The worst amateur paintings *are* these rough and ready paintings, in which the brush strokes come through as if they were made with a rake, and the edges are untidy and wispy, as if the artist was unable to come to grips with the task of getting colours to meet on a canvas.

If you want to work on a tiny scale, do so, but avoid canvas and use cardboard or a smooth surface (not oil-painting paper as that has a marked tooth). Be as precise as you like with your initial design, if necessary using a fine nib (always finer than the sharpest pencil point). Use small soft brushes (00 and 01) throughout, and if you wish make use of a magnifying glass (the type on a heavy stand is the most helpful). It is an odd fact that by using a magnifying glass, the hand seems to acquire the ability to carry out the most minute work. It sometimes happens that the smallest brushes on sale are still not small enough; in which case you will have to adapt one.

There are two ways to do this. The hairs of a brush are fixed to the wooden handle by a metal ferrule. If you gently ease off the ferrule, using the point of nail-scissors or a craft knife, you can take out surplus hairs using eyebrow-tweezers. You

Here the composition begins to gain interest.

The composition complete, with interesting placing of objects.

A rough sketch for 'abstraction' of shapes of the objects.

Zinc White

Lemon Yellow

Cadmium Yellow

Yellow Ochre

Scarlet Lake

Bright Red

Alizarin Crimson

Cerulean Blue

Prussian Blue

Burnt Sienna

An interesting oil painting with detail of the brushwork on the face and hands, which have been under-painted in white in order to bring out the highlights.

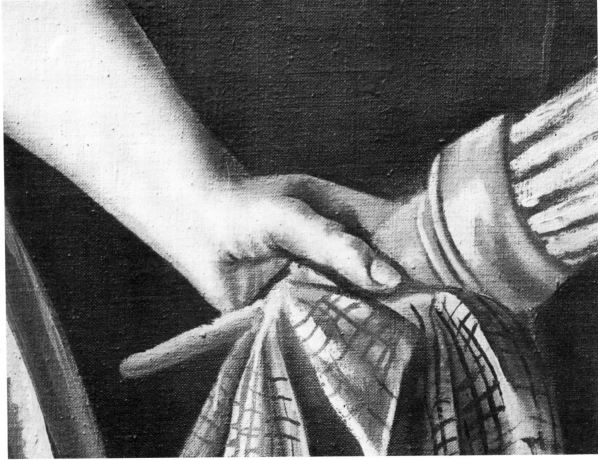

The application of paint with a palette knife.

The technique of scumbling.

The build-up of glazes.

can then replace the ferrule, holding the remaining hairs in the tweezers, tightening the ferrule against the hairs with a pair of pliers. The other method is to cut off surplus hairs close to the ferrule with a razor blade or craft knife (place something between the hairs you want to keep and the superfluous ones before you make the cut).

All techniques can be used in miniature painting. The flat brush method can be employed by working with the smallest flat brushes. You can use successive glazes, and you can underpaint. There are some people who find it difficult to paint on a small scale, and if you are talented in this respect make the most of it. There is nothing that takes the eye more than an exquisite miniature.

The *usual* method of oil painting is to paint in the darks first, and superimpose the half-tones and the lights, and many painters in watercolours also do this, though you will find many writers on watercolour painting not keen on this idea. By putting in the darks first, you immediately get some idea of the shape the picture is taking, and it will give you freedom when you put in the lighter colours, freedom to intrude on the dark areas with your light colours, even mixing in the lights with the darks.

You can apply the paint onto the canvas in many ways. You can take the paint with your palette knife, spread it on the appropriate part of the canvas, and then get to work with your brush. You can load the brush with paint from the palette, and mix on the palette with your medium before going to the canvas. You can apply the paint from the palette onto the canvas, and add the medium to the paint already down. In this case, you will lay the paint down fairly roughly, keeping well within your outlines, only getting your edges in with the arrival of the medium. You can also apply the paint directly from the tube, and indeed some artists use the nozzle of the tube to spread the paint. You have to be very sure of yourself to do this, as it can result in an unholy mess.

If you are not using brushes at all but only palette knives, be sparing of the medium. You can mix your paint on the palette, taking it off with a smooth sweep of the palette knife, or you can squeeze the pure colour on to the palette knife, spread on the canvas, and do the mixing there. Do not try to do palette-knife work with too little paint, but if you want to work up a rich impasto while economizing on paint you can add wax to the mix, a technique used by van Gogh.

If you are using a palette knife or any method involving thick paint any outline drawing you have made will soon disappear, so do not panic if your guide lines suddenly disappear. You can put them back using thin brush strokes, if your paint surface will take them, or you can 'draw' on the paint with the point of a pair of dividers or the wrong end of your brush. Always remember that a painting involves outline and shapes, at least in the initial stages. Adjoining shapes are not sacrosanct; you can 'bite' into them with neighbouring colours. For example, in a landscape one of your trees may seem lifeless and need pepping up with more interesting leafage. There is no necessity to add foliage in foliage colour; you can alter the look of the tree by bringing in sky colour on top of the green, taking out the superfluous green with a small palette knife if the paint is not yet dry.

The versatility of oil paint can never be emphasized enough. There is *nothing* you cannot do with it. You can work over and over again on some passage you do not feel happy about, though in watercolour overworking can show, resulting in a tired picture. Although the Victorian painter Burne-Jones was exceptional in spending five years or more on a single picture, give yourself plenty of time when painting an oil, and if you feel slightly uncertain about the progress of a picture put it to one side for a month or more and then return to it.

There are two types of subject where oils are decidedly the most suitable medium: portraits and interiors. In doing interiors, you can really begin to appreciate the subtle tones you can get with oil paints. It is not a category newcomers bother with very much, which is a pity as it has a lot of potential. It is fun creating imaginary interiors, perhaps building it up from a still life, adding in features against the background, not necessarily mapping them out beforehand. Interiors *are* still lifes.

In doing interiors it is vital to get the perspective right, as you will probably include parts of at least two walls, and maybe ceiling and floor. Parallel lines on the horizontal converge to a vanishing point, as we have seen in the chapter on *Drawing*. Vertical lines also recede to a vanishing point, always on eye level (except for accidental vanishing points which do not apply in interiors). At its simplest, the lines of the ceiling will always go down and the lines of the floor always go up.

In daytime scenes, the strongest light will *always* come from the window. Any areas bordering the window, even if the natural colour is white, will be relatively dark. Get the tones in first, and leave detail until the end, and then be selective, though you can put objects in in fine detail. If the 'real' colours clash, alter them or tone them down. If you want to add mystery, keep some of the interior shrouded in dimness, and suggest articles, giving the viewers something to do.

Portraits often need a lot of working over, because it is not easy to hit on a perfect likeness right away. Some books on painting say that it is more important to get the effect of solidity than a likeness. If you are doing a portrait of a specific person there is no point in it looking like someone else. Some artists prefer to get in the shapes with charcoal, others get right on with the painting, but, as always, it is always a benefit to tint the canvas beforehand. Unless you are very sure of yourself, an underpainting is a help in portraiture (a good mixture for this is green and burnt sienna), and getting in the darks first is invaluable. If you are impatient to get started on the portrait, you can tint the canvas with a wash of acrylic, which will dry almost immediately.

A painting by Van Gogh, showing typical brushwork, colours set side by side in stripes, and always the impression of immediacy.

A vigorous pair of paintings with dynamic changes of texture, from the smoothness of the dress to the angularity of the feathers. The close-up details emphasize these points.

ADVANCED TECHNIQUES

There are basically two methods of painting, in whatever medium. There is the direct method, as advised by the Impressionists but not always practised by them, in which the paint, usually opaque, is put on in one application, and there is the building-up method, in which the paint is put on layer upon layer (in watercolour wash upon wash). The second method is the most time consuming, and an artist can spend months, even years, on a large picture, to the detriment of his output. These pictures may not be very good, but they certainly last, and any Italian Renaissance picture (say from the 13th to the middle of the 16th centuries) is sure of a warm welcome whatever the level of competence.

Painters of that time – and much later – had to be proficient in the art of colour-making as well as picture-making. In 1675 the competent but immensely boring portrait painter Sir Godfrey Kneller employed a man solely to make his colours. The artists' colourman dates from about the middle of the 18th century, and in 1776 a certain Matthew Darly was advertising 'transparent colours for staining drawings.' Reeves introduced small soluble cakes of watercolour in about 1820, followed 10 years or so later by Winsor and Newton, who put their watercolour into pans. In 1847 Winsor and Newton introduced watercolour in tubes.

Renaissance artists not only mixed their own colours, but they prepared their own surfaces, usually panel, often of poplar. They coated the panel with gesso, which provided a sound link between panel and paint, and provided brightness beneath the coats of paint. When this was not wanted, the white was toned down with a wash of transparent yellow (the 'imprimitura'). The main outlines of the forms were transferred from the drawing, using the 'pricking' method. At regular intervals holes were pricked into the drawing, and charcoal was dusted through these holes on to the panel, recreating the design. Or by 'squaring-up', a method much used today, and explained in the chapter on Drawing. The Victorian artist Lord Leighton used the pricking method extensively.

The outlines were then emphasized with grey, black or brown ink or paint using a fine brush or a quill pen, with sometimes hatched strokes put in to indicate modelling. In the 15th century a monochrome wash of grey or brown was applied as an underpainting. Then the successive layers of transparent colour were applied. Duccio (1260–1320) used green underpainting for his flesh sections. Green is the complementary colour of the flesh tints, and when the local colour (the 'real' colour) was introduced this green came through the layer above and provided shadow. It was found that adding grey or brown to the flesh tint could result in a muddy colour. This green wash was allowed to dry, and then overpainted with a transparent wash of 'verdaccio', a mixture of black and

ochre. This wash, in turn, was then left to dry.

The green method was very popular among the Italian artists (but not elsewhere). The next stage was the application of the local colours. The flesh tints were applied in separate hatched strokes, starting with a middle tone, white being added for the lighter parts, and the shadows added last. Hatching was used elsewhere, along with evenly graduated washes. Blues in drapery and skies were underpainted in a light dim blue, and the vivid reds were applied over a wash of red ochre and white. This first wash was deliberately not even, adding variety to the final overpainting.

Elsewhere in Europe similar techniques were being employed. The Flemish painters used a lot of ultramarine in their shadow areas, and a soft green was used under blue, particularly when the draperies were of this colour. Titian (1477–1576) came more than two centuries after Duccio, but he still followed the sequence of underpaintings, except that his handling was far freer, and his underpainting of the flesh (except in the deepest shadow) was *darker* than the overpainting. The underpainting served as a foil to the later layers, and washes of blue and red were applied seemingly at random. In the 16th century there came a de-

Far left, above: A 1981 study of a head in an expressionist style, not unlike that of Van Gogh, though the application of the paint, in flat planes, is the artist's own style.

Far left, below: A detail of the background of the previous picture, showing an extremely subtle use of tones.

A study of fruit, painted in very much a 'flat brush' technique.

mand for clever effects and dramatic light and shade. Instead of an underpainting in transparent browns and greys the whole of the canvas was primed with brown, sometimes verging on black (El Greco was particularly keen on this). The local colours were put in light and weak, built up with brighter colour in a dashing manner. The flesh was begun in pink, modelled with madder and black so that the effect was greyish, then boldly overpainted with light flesh colour. El Greco often dragged a dry brush of the light colour over the underpainting so that contrast is heightened. To give brilliance to his draperies, the underpainting was very light, with a good deal of white mixed in with the local colour.

Rubens (1577-1640) came a century after Titian, and was in a position to see that oil paint becomes transparent in time and that the Italian style of brown underpainting had unforeseen consequences as it was coming through the upper layers. Rubens used a brilliant white ground, toned down with yellow imprimitura, and then he applied a grey underpainting, probably using a sponge dipped in size and ground charcoal. He dragged this across the panel in parallel strokes, not completely covering the imprimitura, so that light paint would stand out better than an all-over grey wash. The underpainting was then carried out in transparent brown.

The flesh tint was laid out thickly on the part to be light, and dragged thinly on the shadow areas, and highlights were applied with pure white. Rubens worked fast, and achieved spontaneity, and may be said to have found a formula that suited him perfectly. Rembrandt (1606-1669) had a formula too – lots of shadow, not much light. He used a medium-brown priming on his grounds, modelling in a greeny-grey colour, much darker than the final light tone, not so dark as the final shadows, and this gloom obliged Rembrandt to rely heavily on the medium and light colours in the concluding stages.

Rembrandt and painters like him paved the way to direct painting ('alla prima'), and after the orthodoxy of the early Italian Renaissance painters there was an eagerness to experiment. Caravaggio (1573-1610), although a generation before Rembrandt, looks forward in his theatricality and tight control to a later age, and he was one of the first to be preoccupied with a perfectly smooth finish, using soft brushes and a thin medium, a technique also used by Velazquez (1599-1660). Vermeer (1632-1675) primed his canvas with a brown-grey mixture made from chalk, lead white, umber and charcoal, and it is possible that instead of the traditional underpainting he began by putting in flat areas of colour.

Watteau (1684-1721) often worked directly on to the canvas, making amendments and alterations as he went along, and working at great speed, using too much medium with his paint, which resulted in the deterioration of his paintings. Many 18th-century painters also wished to work rapidly, especially those society painters for whom the commissions were piling up and for whom guineas were more important than the verdict of posterity. Among these was Sir Joshua Reynolds (1723-1792), whose personal motto should have been 'Anything for Money', and whose influential *Discourses on Art* he disregarded completely.

To speed up the drying process he mixed wax with his paints, and some of his pictures have six or seven layers, put on in any order, each with a different drying rate. No wonder that 200 years on the surface of his pictures looks like crazy paving. Reynolds was primarily a portraitist, and he began his work by putting in a rough circle of white on the grey priming of his canvas. Onto the white he placed his head, working rapidly and not waiting for the colours to dry before applying further paint, either solid or in transparent glazes. After he had done the face, and probably the hands, he would pass the picture on to assistants to do the drapery and background, adding the final touches himself. Reynolds could do a face in a day, and charged on average £210 a picture, the equivalent of close on £5000 today.

Although Thomas Gainsborough (1727-1788) is rated higher now, his pictures averaged £168 each, and although he seems to have painted with sump oil he did have some regard for his public, careful in his choice of paints, and not having his pictures brought back to him by his clients for repainting – one of Reynolds's tiresome chores. Gainsborough blocked in his portraits with thin highly diluted paint, completing the face before turning to the drapery and background. He painted with great

freedom and bravura, but kept his methods sound and rarely bodged.

John Constable (1776-1837) had a different technique altogether. He began with pencil and oil sketches, and when he worked he put in his main masses in an undercoat, bringing in the detail gradually. In order to make certain the painting would hang together, he drastically altered major portions. Often accused of leaving his pictures unfinished, Constable would round off the painting with flecks and stabs of highlight, sometimes applied with the palette knife. Glazes of reds and browns were used to add substance to the foreground, and he paid great attention to his clouds. If you visit the Victoria and Albert Museum in London you can see a large number of his cloud studies; he was one of the first artists to actually look at them. No one merits such close study as Constable. He used the technique of scumbling (dragging a nearly dry brush loaded with white over a layer of paint to get sea or sky effects) extensively. His colour seems so natural and realistic that it is sometimes a shock to realize that the accents in the foreground are in pure vermilion and that the shadows are in fact green. It must be admitted that he sometimes overworked his paintings and that the oil studies have more freshness and verve.

William Turner (1775-1851) was the great adventurer in English oil painting, and there is a world of difference between his early prim architectural subjects and the mystery of his later light-bathed paintings. He was very keen on colour theories, which have worked to the detriment of his paintings as his yellows have proved fugitive and some of his pictures have taken on an arcane quality due to colour changes. In many of his pictures he returned to the white ground of earlier painters, putting in his underpainting in bright pastel colours much diluted with turpentine, applying thick or thin paint on top to get his effect, and for Turner effect was all, and he employed any technique to get it – scumbling, glazing, palette-knife, scratching, diluting thick paint already on the canvas, and even mixing his colours on the canvas rather than on the palette. Often he laid his pure colours down side by side, and it is no wonder that the Impressionists in France claimed Turner as their own. It is difficult to think of any other artist who has exploited the qualities of oil paints so completely as Turner, and if he did have a weak point it was in his figure work.

It was in figure painting that William Etty (1787-1849) was supreme. The nude was Etty's subject and obsession, and he was probably the most 'painterly' specialist artist of the period. Known as the English Titian, Etty was a master of his medium, and in his flesh tints managed to produce a pearly glow so distinctive that it was said that he used a 'secret medium'. Unlike other classically trained painters, Etty employed any technique that occurred to him, taking off glazes with his thumb, dabbing at the paint surface with his pocket handkerchief, and scratching with his thumb nail when it seemed that this was what was

Top: Constable's sketch for 'Hadleigh Castle' shows the vigour and freshness of his studies, qualities sometimes lost in the finished painting. Note how he gets his effect of distance by the simplest of white scumbles.

Above: A charming painting, 'The Path to the Old Ferry at By' by Alfred Sisley, showing colour achieved by dabs and strokes.

picture *The Angelus* was probably the most famous painting in the world. Unending toil was the theme of Millet's work, which was subdued in colour (browns, blue/green, black, white, iron oxide red), and dramatic in lighting. Millet used an off-white priming, and he established his design with charcoal or chalk, using a wash to establish outlines and masses. Shadows were added, leaving the underpainting for the half-tints, and the highlights were added, fairly heavily. The background was often colour-scumbled, letting the underpainting show through, and he strengthened his outlines with a soft brush which although effective at times gives his figures the appearance of cut-outs or cartoon characters; not the kind of thing the Paris art schools liked at all. The texture of Millet's paint closely resembles Polyfilla, but his vigorous handling and unconcern for the proprieties had a powerful effect on subsequent painters, such as van Gogh. He also made gloom and the downtrodden peasantry fashionable. The handling of paint, clotted and earthy, is akin to the techniques used by the 'Kitchen Sink' English school of the 1950s and 1960s. There is no doubt that Millet is an important figure and well worth more than a cursory glance. It is the kind of painting which is not too difficult to do and which always makes a dramatic impact on the spectator.

It is a world away from the academically trained British artists of the period, who thrived on patience and perseverance and techniques of a high order, not afraid to spend weeks on some tiny detail and who used brushes with one or two hairs only. The ultimate in this kind of high-detail work is Richard Dadd's *Titania*, which became the highest priced British painting of all time in March 1983 at £500,000.

You can still hear modern artists sneering at the Victorian painters, even though their work now regularly commands four and five figure sums in the sale room. This may be due to sour grapes because these modern artists cannot emulate the skill and artistry of Victorian painters. You can fudge a Millet, a Constable, or a van Gogh; you cannot fudge a Lord Leighton, an Alma-Tadema, or a Poynter.

Typical of these was Lord Leighton (1830-1896), whose nudes created something of a scandal when they were exhibited at the Royal Academy. Leighton made many thumb-nail sketches before he began, and then laid out his design on paper, squaring it up for transfer to canvas or, if the design was full-size, using the pricking method. A small oil-sketch was made to establish the colour scheme, and then Leighton put in his underpainting in a warm monochrome. If it was a nude the nude was painted first, and the draperies were added later, from separate studies. Leighton used a flat translucent wash for the draperies so that the modelling of the nude would show through, and he then began to apply the thicker colour, preferring stiff paint with very little medium. He kept the surface 'dead' until the latter stages, when he would add more medium to liven the painting up. His colour scheme, about which he was careful,

wanted. He achieved a pearly glow through tiny specks of black and white.

With the increasing number of art schools and the growing influence of the Royal Academy Schools, there was an emphasis on formula painting, tight control, and no improvising. To escape this formal training, many students went to Paris to study in the studios of the famous French artists of the time, only to find that they too were hard taskmasters, though there was always the odd eccentric.

Typical of the 19th-century French painters was Jean Millet (1814-1875), one of a group known disparagingly as the Dismals on account of their subject matter and not their personalities. Millet's

A complete contrast, showing the way art was going, Manet's study of a woman with a cat. Notice the way the paint is applied in diagonal hatching with the highlights applied last of all by delicate flecks of white.

was ultramarine, yellow, cadmium red, scarlet madder, yellow ochre, burnt sienna, indigo, rose madder, madder carmine, black and white. He and his contemporaries preferred a white priming, as this was what his clients liked, as a reaction against the 'Black Masters' (the old painters whose work could barely be discerned beneath their coatings of heavy varnish and dirt). The sparkling character of much Victorian painting owes everything to precise and well-understood techniques, which is still in evidence.

The Victorian academic painters based their pictures on good drawings; oil paintings were regarded largely as tinted drawings, and the greatest public acclaim came for those pictures which were as near to reality as possible, and had finish. There was little wilful distortion, except for comic effect: this was left to the cartoonists and caricaturists. Of course there were some painters, such as Rossetti, who had not trained at the art-world establishments, and others who pursued their ways oblivious to public opinion. G. F. Watts was more concerned with the message and not the medium, and his vast allegorical pictures are still out of

Claude Monet's 'Woman seated on a Bench', showing the loose handling and luminosity characteristic of this artist.

fashion. When he felt that he had made his point, Watts stopped painting his particular picture, and the rough coarse canvas he preferred was left with blank spaces showing through, so sparse was the paint. He laid on pure colours without mixing them on the palette, he ignored detail, and he did not like his objects to have firm outlines, preferring to see them melt into the background.

There were always painters who broke with the establishment, either from inner compulsion to do their own thing or from the awareness that there was no one best way to paint. Edouard Manet (1832–1883) combined traditional and experimental techniques. He was influenced by Velazquez, and wished to reduce half-tone in his pictures and thus stress the contrast between lights and darks. He used off-white canvases, painted wet-on-wet mixing his colours on the canvas, and when he had painted his main groups he defined them by going over the outlines with a pointed brush. His main objects he painted with thick rich pigment, but his backgrounds were often scumbled. Sometimes he would scrape down his day's work, leaving the merest vestiges, and evolve anew from these. Although often lumped in with Impressionists such as Monet, Manet was a supreme virtuoso, knowing instinctively when to leave off, and how to suggest texture without being too specific. If you want an English equivalent, there is no more suitable candidate than John Singer Sargent (who as it happens was American).

Why Manet is still described as an Impressionist is something of a mystery; probably because he gets muddled with Claude Monet (1840–1926), a painter preoccupied with catching the fleeting

effects of light, and who thus had to work fast and on the spot. He used a weak see-through priming, and blocked in his main features with thin scumbled paint, over which he applied opaque paint very dry, dragging the brush across the

This painting, 'Clothes on the Grass' by Seurat, shows the artist simplifying his subject into almost an abstract pattern.

Left, above: With Bonnard, the accent on pattern-making is very obvious and the way is open to the purely decorative artists of the 20th century.

Above: Matisse is typical of the artists of the generation subsequent to Bonnard, in which objects are set on a flat plane and perspective is distorted for pictorial effect.

underpainting in strokes so that the previous layer showed through. There are very few absolute darks in Monet's paintings, for he usually mixed his colours with white. He was good on shimmering effects, and creating texture through his brushwork, often drawing through the paint with the handle of his brush to reveal the colour beneath. Viewing a Monet painting at close range is a meaningless exercise, for we see only dabs and blotches of colour. Despite the speed at which he worked, Monet was always careful with technique, and despite his mixtures of wet-on-wet and wet-on-dry and his indifference, especially in his later work, to outline he managed to avoid muddiness, a constant menace to those who paint in dabs rather than areas of colour.

Georges Seurat (1859–1891) became concerned with colour and optical theory, and introduced the 'pointillist' technique, covering the painted areas with tiny dots of different colours, which, in theory, merge in the viewer's eye to become one. He painted wet-over-dry to retain the vivacity of the colours, and in his underpainting, carried out in the local colours of the objects, he outlined the objects with the brush. His object outlines are always immaculately defined, and his areas are never blurred and haphazard. His colour sense was incredibly subtle, which cannot be said of his almost exact contemporary Vincent van Gogh (1853–1890), whose *Sunflowers* has probably inspired many amateur artists, often with disastrous consequences. Van Gogh used coarse canvases, often painting directly on to them without a priming, and using opaque paint from the start, without any attempt at underpainting. The features of his pictures were worked over and outlined, usually in an unlikely colour such as blue or brown. The texture of van Gogh's paint has something of cream cheese, and to build up his impasto he mixed in wax. There was no attempt at finish, and his vigorous and frenzied brushwork is everywhere evident. In his admirers this type of brushwork becomes scratchy and irritating.

In his way, van Gogh emancipated colour from the restrictions placed on it by reality, and in the beginning of the 20th century a group of painters known as the Fauves ('wild beasts') glorified paint, were not concerned with representation, painted directly, and, like van Gogh, drew lines around their subjects to define them rather than let the paint areas do this job. Characteristic of these painters was Henri Matisse, but it was probably the type of artist personified by Pierre Bonnard (1867–1947) who has had more influence on more recent representational art. Bonnard was not interested in building up solidity or creating an illusion of depth, but aimed at a tapestry effect. He used a fairly absorbent ground, applied thin scumbles of diluted paint which he then intensified with thicker dabs of dryish powdery paint, a subtle form of picture-making which had its parallels in England.

We have the paradox of artists using conventional means to paint unconventional pictures (even early Picasso of the Cubist period fits into this category) and artists using unconventional means to paint conventional pictures. A splendid example is the Newlyn School of Cornwall, which flourished from about 1885. Their techniques, especially those of the key artist Stanhope Forbes, would not seem at all outrageous today – indeed, their methods were wholeheartedly taken up by art colleges in later years. The Newlyn painters were very keen on outdoor painting – 'Your work cannot really be good unless you have caught a cold doing it' one of the artists commented wryly –

Jean Dubuffet's 'Spinning Round' (1961), painted in a deliberately child-like style and having its own kind of niche.

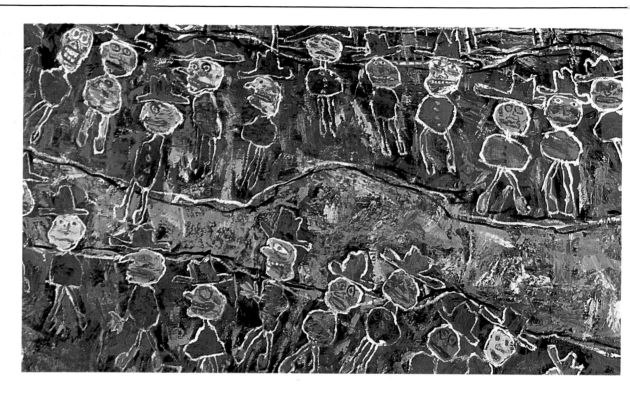

but this had nothing to do with the technique they began to use, which the critics thought was derived from France.

This was the use of flat square soft brushes, a technique that was ridiculed by the critics in the late 1880s, though it had been used for well over a decade, especially by Stanhope Forbes (1857–1947). The painters of the 'Square Brush School' concentrated on tone, outlines were blurred, and the evocation of atmosphere was encouraged. The strokes were crisscrossed and hatched. An excellent description of the difference between standard technique and square brush was written by a critic in 1893:

> 'The technique of the Newlyner is often thus roughly described: the ordinary, everyday artist, if he wants to paint a ship's mast against the sky, takes a brush, coming to a fine point, and draws it vertically up and down his canvas in the place desired. The Newlyner does nothing of the sort. He uses a squarer brush and gets his mast by series of horizontal strokes.'

Stanhope Forbes gradually gave up his concern with tone rather than colour from about 1910 when he was elected a Royal Academician. The square brush style of painting certainly did not exclude detail, though the more modern practitioners of the method took the same delight in tone rather than colour, as we can see in the 'descendants' of the Newlyn School, the Euston Road School, the London Group, and the Camden Town School – and, sometimes incongruously, in contemporary painters who happened to be at art school when this technique was being most arduously advocated.

With the breakdown of traditional art teaching, the way has been left open to the most fantastic of methods, some good, some not so good. The seeds of anarchy were sewn (for good rather than for ill

as Edwardian painting was getting stale) in the first two decades of this century, when the artist began to explore all the possibilities, introducing into his paintings elements from outside, such as sticking on bits (collage). At its most extreme, collage could incorporate vegetable matter, as with Jean Dubuffet's work; in the 1960s I saw one of his pictures begin to disintegrate in the hot atmosphere of an exhibition gallery. If modern art has done nothing other than encourage timid amateurs to have a go, it has provided a service.

Modern art is popularly supposed to be progressive or futuristic, but of course this is not necessarily so, nor are the most inventive of contemporary painters less careful in their techniques than the artists of previous centuries. Naturally the more outrageous artists get the attention of the media, but a lot of noise and publicity does not mean that they are any good, and will not be forgotten in 20 years time. Many of the so-called pathfinders to a new art have disappeared entirely from view.

Of the 20th-century artists about whose credentials there is no doubt, Paul Klee stands out. He also explained his techniques with extreme lucidity in *Paul Klee on Modern Art* (1948). He wrote about how he started a picture by doodling, by playing with lines and colours until they suggested some association or title; he mentions 'lines going for a walk'. Sometimes a title preceded the actual work; usually it was an enigmatic or fairy-tale title, a label that often had little to connect it with the actual picture. It is often difficult to say which is playing the greater part in Klee's work, the conscious or the unconscious. Except in his later paintings when he was inclined to be turgid, the bulk of his work is enchanting, small-scaled, and rich in detail and texture – and without modelling of any kind.

A detail from 'They're Biting' by Paul Klee (1920). Klee often put enigmatic titles to his pictures, but this one is succinct and logical. One of the best of Klees, it well illustrates his idea of 'lines going for a walk' – and what an expressive line it is!

David Hockney has brought precision and an immaculate technique to bear on this painting of Mr and Mrs Ozzie Clark (and Percy the cat). Notice the perfect placement of the various adjuncts to the main subjects.

In *The Refugee*, Klee used six distinct media and as many as 10 layers. Working on cardboard, he first of all applied a priming of white, then reinforced the surface with gauze, glue and gesso. He then did an underpainting in brown watercolour, then put in his design with tempera, refining this with detailed drawing and watercolour hatching. He then put on a coat of thin varnish, and then heightened certain details with white oil paint. He then put on a glaze of blue-grey oil colour, and when this had dried finished off the painting with a glaze of madder lake. Sometimes he built up his paintings like mosaics, with hundreds of tiny squares of contrasting colour. Klee was one of the least brash of 20th-century artists; Roy Lichtenstein, the American pop artist, was probably one of the most.

It is interesting to compare the way Klee and Lichtenstein dealt with their surface textures, in particular their dots of paint. Klee's dots were applied individually; Lichtenstein, with the aim of getting the look of a comic or of a half-tone reproduction in a newspaper, used a metal mesh screen, which was placed on the canvas. Paint was brushed through the circular holes, and the screen was lifted off.

While pop art unquestionably has its niche, irritating as it may be to those not turned on by comic strips or Marilyn Monroe, many of the better artists of today have returned to representation, and some of them, such as Peter Blake, have very assured techniques that equal those of the best Victorian artists. In his more recent work, David Hockney paints with the care and precision, the preparation and attention to detail, that was expected of the masters of the past, using traditional techniques in acrylic rather than oil paint, and demonstrating that this medium is not as crude as many of us are inclined to think.

However, this is not an art history or a paean to selected artists. Can we learn from these techniques? Although many of us are too impatient to apply glaze after slow-drying glaze over a carefully designed underpainting, we can short-circuit the oil-painting process by using acrylic, in which five successive glazes will dry in a couple of hours. One of the virtues of the use of transparent glazes is that the picture comes along bit by bit, underpinned by the underpainting so that the artist who has some idea of the end product cannot come wholly to grief. Painting direct *can* be a hit-or-miss method, though it is unquestionably the method most practised today.

For those who wish to simplify their forms, or are more concerned with colour than with tone or reality, there is a lot to be said for the black-line method (outlining the objects in a picture, or some of the primary objects in a picture, with the point of a soft brush). At its most subtle, this method can be seen in the work of Matisse; at its most majestic and sombre in the work of Georges Rouault. Rouault painted in several layers, altering and amending, outlining his paint areas with thick black lines. He then continued to overpaint the exposed portions, until the paint areas stood as much as an inch high from the encircling boundaries. When he was praised by a friend for this impasto, Rouault replied: 'But I do not want it at all, I just can not stop overpainting again and again.' A modern art historian perceptively drew an analogy between Rouault's paintings and stained glass windows.

The black-line method need not be forceful and attention-grabbing, but merely a faint line separating the various patches of colour, a process used for centuries, particularly in watercolour painting. There is no question that there are more technical variations possible in oil painting than in watercolours, simply because of the plasticity of the medium.

Watercolour painting is older than oil painting, and was used by monks for illustrating manuscripts before they found that gouache, mixing their watercolour pigments with white, provided a better base for the inevitable gold embellishment. In the 17th century Dutch painters added a little colour to their drawings to liven them up; tinted drawings then became fashionable, the colours limited to blue, yellow, green, brown and rose madder. Among the first English artists to use the tinted drawing style was Francis Barlow (1626–1702). Watercolours were not regarded as at all important, but were records, notes for oil paintings, or sketches for engravings. Early paper was thin and fragile, and artists were obliged to scrape them to make them serviceable. Many artists made their own ink, sepia or black, and diluted them so that they could supplement pen-and-ink work with a thin ink wash.

Topographical artists commonly used a single wash, but the more adventurous found there were great possibilities in several washes, and different ways of applying paint, in dabs as used by David Cox or stippling where the paint is applied in the form of dots, as exploited by Birket Foster in innumerable village cottage scenes. Lifting the colour from the paper to expose highlights was done extensively by using rag, india-rubber, blotting paper, or dry bread. Francis Nicholson anticipated the use of masking fluid by applying a mixture of turpentine, beeswax and white, over which he painted his washes. When the wash had dried, he would lift his mixture with turpentine.

Shadows were put in with Prussian blue and brown ink, and later by darker tones of the local colour. John Sell Cotman and Turner achieved their highlights by taking off the wet paint with the wooden end of the brush. This left a hard dark edge by creating a kind of canal at the edge of the highlight, an effect impossible to get with the brush and less brutal than lifting the colour off with a knife. John Varley's device was to paint upon thin paper laid on white card, and when he wanted a highlight he would scratch right through the paper so that the white of the card would show through.

Varley (1778–1842) was very influential, and he introduced another widely copied technique: he placed masses of colour with little pencil drawing, and separated them by thin white lines. John

Detail from a landscape by Cozens, the Lake of Albano and Castel Gandolfo, well illustrating the 18th-century preoccupation with the evocation of distance.

English Impressionism is epitomized by Steer. Although at times he was inclined to be sketchy, this study of girls at the seaside bears comparison with the work of his French contemporaries.

Glover (1767-1849) is little known today but invented a short cut in doing foliage by making a 'split brush' (binding together the hairs to make several points) so that he could economize on time and effort. Glover did his skies in a mixture of indigo and Indian red, which have faded badly.

Those watercolour artists who also did engravings found that they could duplicate drawings very well by taking blacklead impressions from an etched plate. It was very convenient for those who worked to a formula. Each watercolourist had his favourite colour scheme; John Cozens (1752-1797) used a basic palette of greys and blues with a very restricted use of brighter colours. John Webber (1750-1793) used blues, greys and light yellows.

Many 19th-century artists applied the paint to the paper without pencil drawings, using the splashes and blobs as a basis for a composition, others used rich watercolour to make a mosaic, and others returned to the tinted drawing format, with a difference. The work of Arthur Rackham and Edmund Dulac is a token of what can be done in book illustration and as superb watercolour paintings in their own right. Watercolour lends itself equally to atmospheric suggestiveness or precision, and can do almost anything required.

CHAPTER 3

WATERCOLOURS AND GOUACHES

WHAT ARE WATERCOLOURS?

Pigment mixed with a gum which acts as a binder; this binder is soluble in water. The traditional gum was gum arabic (which naturally came from Arabia) but it has been largely replaced by gum from a species of acacia tree grown in Africa. Gouache or opaque watercolour varies in quality from ordinary distemper to designers' colour.

WHAT MATERIALS ARE NEEDED?

Watercolours come in tubes or pans, sold in sets or separately. Artists' colours are a good deal more expensive than students' colours, which can be slightly grainy (though this can be an advantage as it provides interesting textures). Opaque watercolours, under whatever name, are sold in tubes, pans or jars; designers' colours are the best, though poster paint sold in jars is useful for covering large areas as it is cheaper. White gouache is sometimes known as process white and is sold in jars, and is extremely useful for eradicating mistakes on pen-and-ink work and pencil drawings. It can also be used to accompany ordinary transparent watercolour, either to provide highlights or as a mix, when it is known as body colour. Watercolour in tubes is very concentrated, and a little goes a long way. For outdoor work a paint box with pans is probably best.

Mediums Normally the only medium needed is water, but gum arabic can be added, and so can megilp, which gives added brilliance and retards the drying.

Varnish Watercolours are not usually varnished, though there is no reason why they should not be. Watercolour varnish is sold in bottles, but there is a considerable danger of taking the colour off when applied even with the softest of brushes and an aerosol varnish is safer. Gouache paintings can be varnished with oil-colour varnishes, but care should be taken and only a soft brush used.

Brushes If treated well, brushes will last for years. Cheap brushes (ox hair, camel hair, etc) are a false economy, though nylon brushes are not, and can equal sable. Do not stint on the number of brushes in your watercolour kit, and get a good range from size 00 upwards, including pointed brushes, flat square brushes, and the long thin brushes known as 'liners' (used for drawing lines but ideal for any kind of detailed work). 'Fan' brushes are also a great help, excellent for blending in washes. To test a pointed brush wet it, shake out the excess water, and roll it on the palm of the hand to form a point. If the point is thin and weak, reject it; if there is too much 'belly' the brush may hold too much water and be difficult to handle. If any hairs come out during this test, the brush is past redemption. Oil-painting brushes can also come in useful, and so can old toothbrushes (which give a good 'splatter' effect) and shaving brushes, for texture and for loading a paper with plenty of water.

Palettes Paint boxes usually have three depressions in the lid to serve as a palette, but these are not very practical, and divided dishes are better. As you will not be standing up to paint with watercolour (and therefore you will not need an easel) the dish for your paint should be by your hand rather than in it. Tin and plastic containers divided into up to eight sections are excellent, but ordinary household saucers can be used, as well as dinner plates. Watercolour mixes best on pottery or china.

Paper Watercolour paper comes in different weights and textures, and also colours (which are fast and will not wash out). A good medium paper is 60-pounds; at 200-pounds it approximates to cardboard. The surfaces of paper are known as 'hot-pressed', which is very smooth, 'not' (not hot-pressed), which is medium, and 'rough', which has a very marked tooth. Unless the paper is thick (above say 72-pounds) sketching blocks are not altogether suitable as the paper is apt to bubble up. Watercolour board, which sometimes goes under the name of fashion board, is usually smooth, and of excellent quality, suitable for all finishes. Cartridge paper is much cheaper than watercolour paper, but unless of good quality is inclined to let the user down, as it puckers up if there is too much water. You can use watercolour paper as it is, pinned to a drawing board, but the best method, though it may take a little extra time, is to 'stretch' it, not nearly so formidable as it sounds. Purists make use of a stretching frame, but far simpler is the method where you wet the paper, lay it on the drawing board face up, and tape it down with masking tape (sellotape is all right but is inclined to tear the paper immediately beneath it). When dry the paper will be drum-tight, a perfect working surface, and if need be the paper can be dampened slightly again before painting. Stretching is more necessary when the paper is light. A further short cut is to dampen the paper and fix it to the drawing board with spring clips (sold by art shops). For outdoor work where you may not need paper drawing-board size, a smaller panel of wood can suffice, and where you intend making several pictures you can put down several sheets of paper, wetting the top one in turn, painting on it, and then taking it off, leaving the others in the clip for further work.

Drawing Board There is no substitute for a drawing board when painting in watercolours. If you wish to have a more resilient surface, you can place a pad of newspaper between the paper and the board. A *T-square* is an accessory to a drawing board that saves measuring up when you are drawing horizons, and a *Set-square* used in co-ordination with

Stretching paper is essential for achieving a final flat surface for a watercolour. You can either sponge the paper wet or leave it to soak in a sink or bath. It is advisable to cut the gum strip into appropriate lengths before you commence stretching.

Soaking the paper.

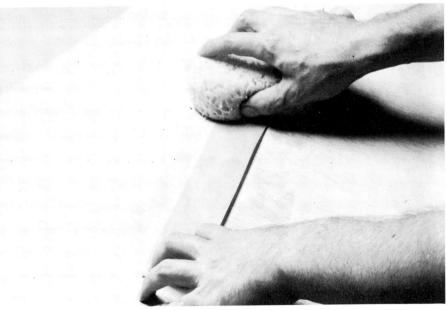

Wetting the pre-cut gum strip.

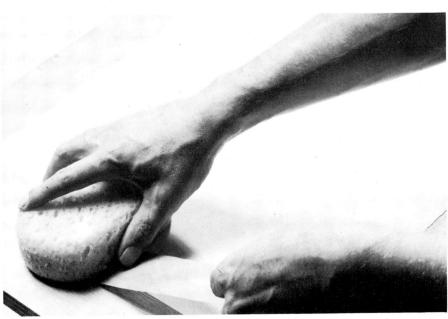

Applying the gum strip to the edge of the paper.

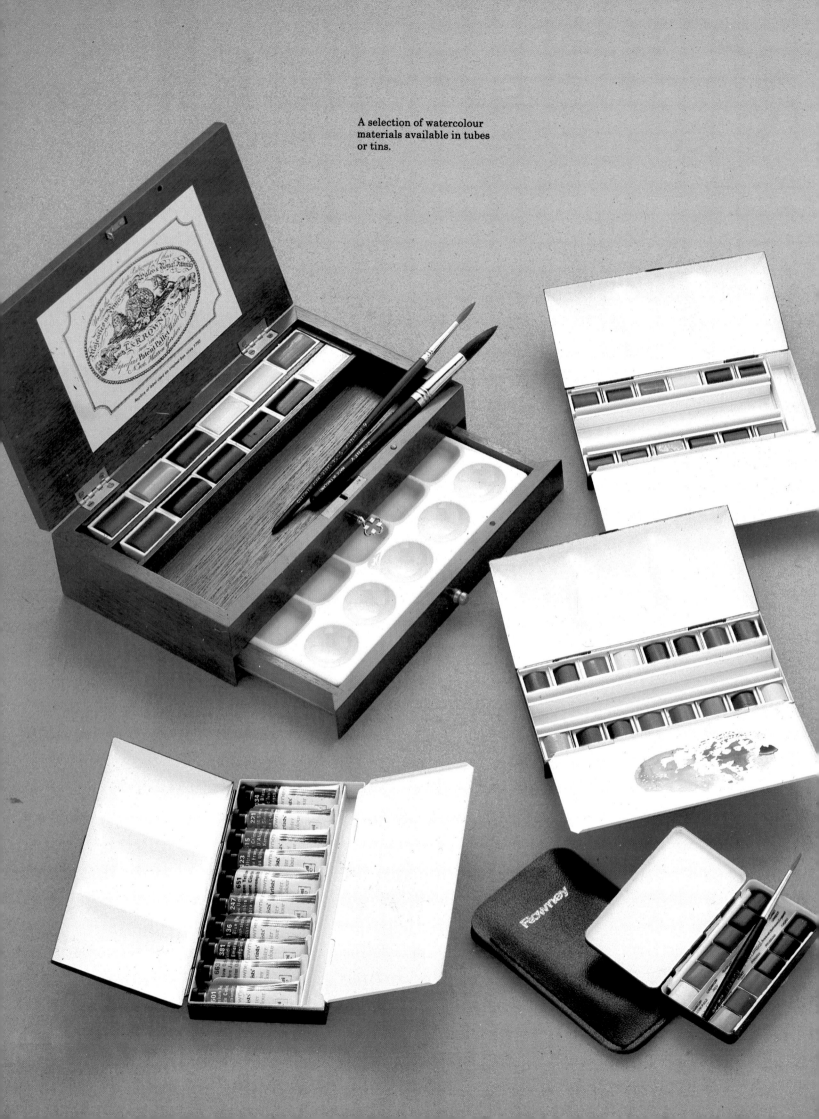

A selection of watercolour
materials available in tubes
or tins.

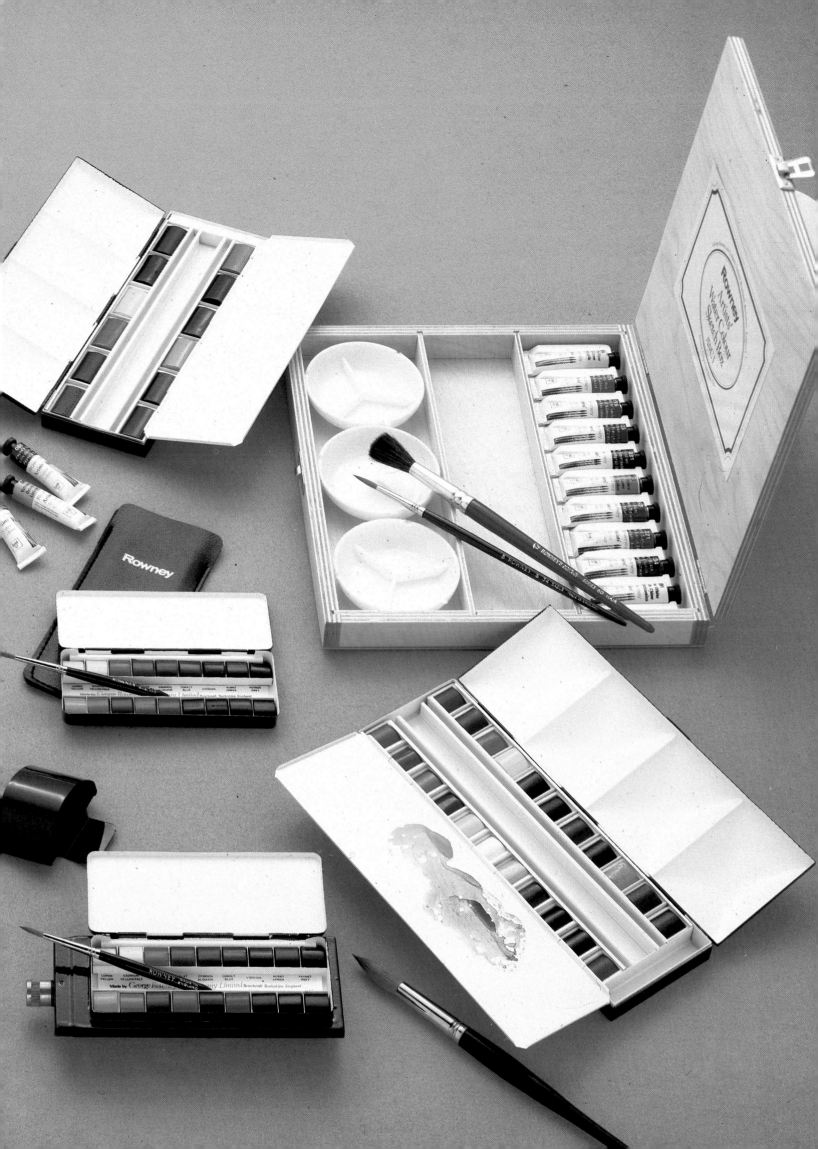

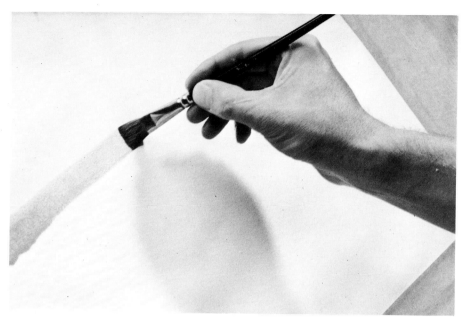

Applying paint with a fully loaded brush.

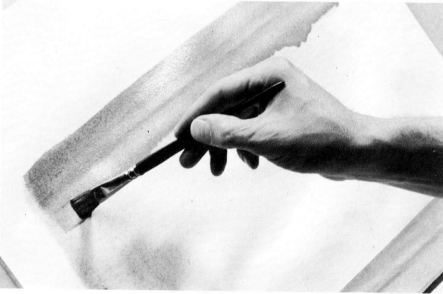

Applying the wash gradually.

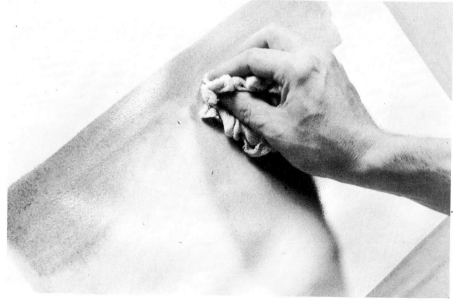

Dabbing with a soft rag or blotting paper.

a T-square will enable you to get your verticals absolutely upright.

You will add other ingredients to your basic kit as you find them necessary, some of them obvious such as *pencils* (a variety from hard to soft), *charcoal* (which mixes well with watercolour), *pastels* (which mix if water-based, and can be used for special effects if oil-based), *dividers* and a pair of *compasses* (an intended circle which is not quite right sticks out like a sore thumb). *Blotting-paper* can be very handy, both to soak up a watercolour wash which has got out of hand, to take out areas (creating clouds in sky and waves in water) and to tone down colours. *Sponge* is also a help in evolving textures, taking out surplus water, and applying paint where the use of a brush is not suitable (where you want a mottled finish). Just as you can use tissue-paper when tonking oil paintings, so you can do much the same thing with blotting paper in watercolour paintings. For fine work, *cotton buds* are excellent to take off surplus moisture. Although there is not much mess associated with watercolours, household tissues and rags are useful.

You can use coloured inks in association with watercolour, therefore *pens* with nibs of different sizes, *Indian* and *coloured inks* should all be kept in mind and within reach, as well as containers for water.

The most important thing in watercolour painting is to know how to apply a wash. There is nothing easier. A wash is a smooth and even transparent tone of diluted colour. You need to have sufficient colour mixed, because you will rarely get the same tint again if you run out half-way. Use a large brush, fully loaded, and with the paper at modest slant (a book under the back of the drawing board is ample), carry the brushful of colour lightly across the top of the paper, left to right, or right to left, but keep the direction consistent. The wet colour will gently roll down like a wavelet, and when it gets to the bottom, or the place you want it to stop, mop off the surplus wash with a dry brush or blotting paper. If you want to graduate your colour, darker at the top, lighter at the bottom, you will add water to your brush after each line of wash so at the bottom you will be using almost pure water. This is excellent for skies. If you want washes darker at the bottom than the top, start with water and add the wash gradually or, alternatively, simply turn your paper upside-down. You can introduce washes of a different colour into a wash in progress, or even touches of pure colour from the tube or pan.

If you wish to apply a wash over a large area such as a sky it is advantageous to wet the paper beforehand with a sponge, waiting till it is just moist before applying the wash (you can hurry up the drying process by dabbing with a clean rag). Rough paper will take more water than smooth, and watercolour board least of all. You can lay a wash over a small area, and the only thing to remember is to keep the direction of the brush strokes consistent, and never, for a wash, up and down. Once a wash has been applied, it is better to let it dry out thoroughly before doing anything else, and it is more effective to put strong washes over weak ones than the other way about. You can apply as many successive washes as you want, but after four or so there is a chance of them becoming lifeless as the watercolour paper begins to disappear.

Sometimes you may wish to lay an 'incomplete' wash, a wash where there are objects to be painted which are *lighter* than the wash. The beauty of the colour wash is that it is smooth. You do not want to go round the edges of anything. On the other hand, if this feature is to be lighter than the wash, there will be no way through the wash except by adding white to the mix and making it opaque. This is where masking fluid can be so invaluable. Masking fluid is a creamy sticky substance which you paint on to the area you do not wish to be covered by the wash with a small soft brush. It rapidly becomes tacky, and then dry, and you can apply your wash over it. When the wash is dry, you peel off the masking fluid, either with the point of a knife or by rubbing it with the finger tips, whereupon it will come off like rubber solution. Beneath it the virgin paper will be ready to be painted on. Masking fluid is most suitable on smooth surfaces, as it is inclined to pick up fragments from rough or hairy paper.

When using watercolours it is always advisable to have at least three jars of water, one clean for light washes, one fairly clean, and a general purpose jar for washing out the brushes. If you are using a paint box with pans, there will always be certain pans with vestiges of other colours on them, as at some stage you will mix the colours on your brush rather than in a dish, especially if you are using the colours at full or moderate strength. It is a good idea to clean off the pan surfaces periodically, so that the colour is what it purports to be.

It is quite possible to paint a watercolour using washes only, and indeed many of the great watercolourists of the past have done just that, overlapping the washes to suggest shadow and distance and not needing anything stronger such as paint straight from the pan. Many of these early artists never used white as a colour, preferring to use the white of the paper showing through for their highlights. This was known as 'the English style'. 'The French style', somewhat frowned upon, incorporated white paint – though it might be mentioned that the Chinese white found in most paint boxes is not a very powerful covering agent; process white or designers' white gouache is much more effective.

Most teach-yourself-painting books advise using watercolours light to dark, as opposed to oils where dark to light is reckoned the better. Of course you cannot make much of an impact with light washes over dark washes, even if they can be seen, but despite all this watercolours *can* be used putting the darks in first provided the very dark colours are not used thickly. A wash of brown or diluted black can easily be modified when need be, though it may be necessary to dispel another taboo

– that freshness is all in watercolours, and that the spontaneous touch is a must. This is not so. You can use the technique you want, and you can even modify the 'flat brush' technique of oil painting by rubbing the moist watercolour surface horizontally with the flat sable or nylon brush to get the same kind of texture you can achieve with oils. When you do this naturally you will not be able to use the white of the paper; so you will use white gouache for your highlights.

Watercolour straight from the pan or tube, with just enough water to make the paint flow easily, provides a satisfying counterpoint to washes already laid down. Watercolour paintings do not have to be loose and dreamy; they can be as tight and highly coloured as you like, and the textures can be worked up as diversely as in an oil painting, a prospect that would have horrified the 18th-century masters of the medium, especially those who worked to a formula and whose pictures now fetch big money simply because of the art market. One of these archaic formulas was to tint the paper according to the mood of the picture – nearly always a landscape. A wash of Naples yellow or yellow ochre was applied for a sunny lyrical scene, and a wash of grey or natural tint gave the right sense of foreboding for an overcast scene. There is nothing against this dodge – in fact it can make sense today – but it should not become a habit.

Textures add interest to the picture surface, and there are many ways to achieve this. An interesting method is spattering the wash (still moist or dry) by loading a bristle brush with paint and running the fingers quickly through the bristles. You can put dots of colour by using a loaded decorator's brush and dabbing the tips of the bristles on to the surface. You can create the impression of foliage by dabbing at a green area with a sponge, blotting paper or tissues. A feathery texture can be achieved by holding a large brush, with not much paint on, close to the end of the bristles, and flicking the paper. The character of watercolour can be changed completely by being covered with blotting paper while still wet, and an even more drastic way is to immerse the watercolour in a bowl of water, swirl the paper slightly, take out, and treat with blotting paper. A watercolour which seems to be getting dull can be transformed by the use of pen-and-ink, pastel, coloured pencils, and gouache. Gouache and true watercolour do not need to exist in self-contained compartments, but can be blended perfectly well on the same sheet of paper.

In laying a sequence of orthodox washes it *is* advisable to let each wash dry out in turn; however remarkable effects can be obtained by painting wet-on-wet, guiding the changing colours with blotting paper. Paint straight from the pan can be put down moist, and then a loaded brush of water is placed gently on top. Once again as you watch to see how chance is operating you have blotting paper or a tissue at the ready to control it. There is no way to predict how one colour will 'bleed' into another, but manipulating the transition takes away the element of chance.

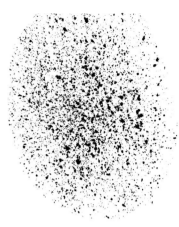
Flicking paint brush.

Dabbing with decorator's brush.

Dabbing over wash with tissue.

Dabbing dry wash with sponge.

Dabbing wet wash with sponge.

Right and below: A gradual build up of washes (notice that areas of paper have been left open) for sky and clouds, finished with small applications of thicker white paint.

Far right, top: Here, the cloud formations are painted with thicker white paint over a complete blue wash.

Far right, bottom: A light wash, with subtle washes of darker colour for clouds, creates a dramatic, but not overworked, sunset effect. Notice how the 'edges' of the clouds are highlighted with yellow. It is important to remember that clouds are not flat; they have a form and will therefore react to light.

Building up a seascape,
working from a photograph.
The different areas are
roughly sketched out and
the various washes applied.
Finally, the buildings and
the boats are added, albeit in
a simplified form.

There are so many ways of experimenting with watercolour that you will find your own method, and if you think you have discovered a winner go ahead with it despite failures, changing your brushes, changing the colours you are using, or turning to a different kind of paper. It is a far cry from the overlapping washes of the old masters, but they too were not averse to experiment, without having the variety of brushes, colours and papers that we have today.

All the methods described have been different ways of applying ordinary watercolour paint to the surface of the paper, but any outside medium, such as water-based pastels (or coloured pencils), are compatible with watercolour. By using the incompatibility of oil and water we can get amazing results. Mention has already been made of the technique of using oil pastels in combination with watercolour, and this can be extended to using candle grease. If you stroke a candle across paper you will lay down a film, and when this is painted with watercolour the paint will slip off it or it will lie on top, unable to penetrate to the paper. Candle grease will not take the top off a wash, and when applied further washes will in all probability flow off it or settle uneasily on top, depending on how much candle grease you have put on. A further variation is pitting the layer of candle grease, either with a sharp object or by rubbing it with sandpaper. Where the paper is exposed the watercolour will take. Use the candle method with discretion; you are not making a candle-grease pie.

IS THE WATERCOLOUR WASH THE VERY FIRST STEP TO A PAINTING?

It can be – if for example you are going to have a large expanse of sky – but not necessarily. You may wish to outline your design on the white paper, and then put in the first wash. At the other extreme, you may not want to put in *any* design, not even rough pencil marks to show what is going where.

If you want to do a watercolour painting which is virtually a tinted drawing you put all your detail in, either with a sharp pencil or pen and ink, remembering that if you want additional effect and the ink to 'bleed' into the watercolour you must use non-waterproof ink.

A simple exercise which will give you a chance to try out a simple wash is that outlined in the chapter on oil painting – a sea scheme with a ship. Draw a horizontal line about two-thirds of the way down the paper, used upright or lengthwise. Apply your wash of diluted blue (ultramarine or Prussian blue), darker at the top, and stop it at the horizon, using blotting paper or tissue. If it overlaps slightly it does not matter as your sea will be darker than your sky. Mix a sea-colour wash, using what seem to be appropriate colours; blue and green are the obvious ones, but add other colours, such as a brown and, for extra drama, a

Working from a colour transparency. Notice how the artist has altered the 'wide angle' look of the original and made the perspective more realistic.

Manganese Blue

Manganese Blue/Vandyke Brown

Vandyke Brown

Vandyke Brown/Purple Lake/Cadmium Red

Cadmium Red

Purple Lake

Sap Green/Cobalt Green

Raw Sienna/White

Gouache and water colour as washes can be combined successfully with pen and waterproof ink to add colour and depth to a drawing.

A simple seascape, using washes and flecks of white paint.

A dramatic landscape or moorland.

Manganese

Sap Green

Cobalt Green

Vandyke Brown

Vandyke Brown/Sap Green

Raw Sienna

Sap Green/Cobalt Green

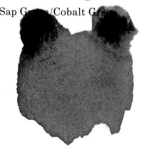

Manganese Blue/Vandyke Brown

A slightly abstracted landscape, using plenty of colour and washes.

The stages to be followed in painting a watercolour of a bridge, working from a photograph.

touch of black. Lay down your wash from the horizontal line, letting the water go to the bottom of the paper and there mopping up the surplus. At any stage during this wash you can add further colours.

If you wish to have clouds, prod at the blue wash while still moist with a pad of cotton wool. If you wish to have waves on the water use the edge of a piece of blotting paper, picking out wave shapes, but not excessively, indicating rather than describing. You can mix a darker wash, perhaps brown with a touch of blue, and put in land on the horizon, adding variety by giving light and shade with a small piece of blotting paper or a cotton bud. If you want a darker piece of land use paint straight from the pan. Unless the land is going to be elaborate you can place this in without preliminary drawing, though the boat will probably have to be drawn in (or traced in). It is easier to have the boat on the horizon, straddling the horizon, or not far below it, because if it is near the bottom of the paper you will be looking down on it, and the boat shape will not be so evident to a viewer. If you are tracing a boat on to the paper

bear its logical position in mind. If the sky is fairly light you will find that birds in white will not show up very clearly, though they will on a green/blue sea. You can pick the bird shapes out (a flat V) with blotting paper, adding a touch of black at the front end to indicate the head and beak. Or you can put the sea-birds in with opaque white paint, such as process white. It must be emphasized that the Chinese white found in paint-boxes is *not* a very solid covering pigment.

A second simple picture can be made using the example mentioned in the oil-painting chapter – hills, a middle distance of trees and a pond in the foreground. As before, you put the horizon in, and you can then put in the whole of the sky, even over the part where the hills will come (the hill colour will go over the sky colour). For relatively simple shapes, you may not need to pencil in the outlines, or you may prefer to put them in using some kind of neutral tint and a pointed brush. The darkest area of the picture will be the line of trees between hills and pond, and you can experiment with reflections, adding tiny dots of pure colour to suggest people. Remember that reflections are always

The development of a water-colour showing a group of palm trees.

Manganese Blue

Windsor Blue

Olive Green

Gamboge Yellow

Hooker's Green

Permanent Mauve

Burnt Sienna

Neutral Tint

absolutely vertical. For the hill part, you can apply further washes to suggest where the light is falling, or you can take out some of the first wash with blotting paper. You can also use blotting paper to take out clouds (and reflections of clouds). In the line of trees, try not to make them too green, adding brown or red to cool the colour down.

If you wish to try your hand at more detailed work, put in grasses and reeds in the immediate foreground, suggesting that this is the limit of the pond, and you can use fairly strong colour for such features. When you have got the basic picture down, and are reasonably happy with it, do not be afraid to experiment. If you do not quite know *what* to put in, look through some illustrations; there will certainly be something suitable, and if you do not feel sufficiently confident to put in a detailed object try a blocked-in silhouette, remarkably effective against a background. From the start cultivate a spirit of adventure, and if you feel that you are on to something persist with it. Forget the old chestnut that watercolours should have a feeling of freshness and spontaneity about them. The Victorian watercolours that fetch such huge sums in salerooms are precisely those that are well-worked, without any spontaneity. This is one reason why it is a good idea to use good quality watercolour paper, which stands a lot of punishment – rubbing out, overpainting, scratching out, everything.

The exercises mentioned above will not do very much to refine your sense of *tone*. The kind of painting which allows delicate gradations of tone is typified by the still life. This can be imaginary – it is no difficult matter to visualize bottles, jars, and the odd apple or lemon – or from life. Bottles are useful as they have highlights, which appear on the same side as the light source.

The simplest kind of still-life painting is carried out by covering the whole paper with a tint, then sketching objects in roughly with a pencil, charcoal, or the point of a brush. The paper will still be slightly moist, so do not worry if the outline design (if done with the brush) bleeds into the background. Then using a medium wash for each object, making certain that the colours do not clash too much, fill in the objects, defining the bottle shapes, jars and fruit. This should not take long, and before the paint is too dry take out the highlights of the various items with a damp brush, again not worrying if the colour slops over. For darker objects, apply further washes, either of the same colour or some other, skirting round the highlights you have put in. If the paper is still moist, this helps merge the colours.

You now have four tones, including the highlights, and you provide a fifth, with shadow, which need not necessarily be black. Brown plus blue makes an excellent shadow mix. You can leave the outlines fairly loose if you wish, or you can tidy them up, either by applying further washes on the objects, applying a further wash on the background, using a small brush to run along the edge of the bottles, or you can tidy up by using a wet

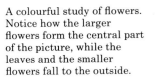

A colourful study of flowers. Notice how the larger flowers form the central part of the picture, while the leaves and the smaller flowers fall to the outside.

The step-by-step development of a mountainous landscape, showing a detail (*bottom left*) of the brush-work. Mountains are an ideal subject for watercolour as various strengths of washes can be used to denote distance.

brush and taking off the wash where it has leaked over into an adjacent area. If you wish, you can use white to provide highlights rather than the white of the paper. This, of course, is the traditional light-to-dark method.

Rather than start off again, you can take off the paint with a wet sponge, or put the paper under a tap, so that you have the merest skeleton of your original watercolour painting. You can then go from dark-to-light, putting in your shadows first, your next darkest tints, and so on back to the background, putting in highlights with white paint last of all. If you are used to oil painting this method will come easily. For the whole of the painting you can make do with one brush, a medium about number three, pointed.

After inanimate objects, it is tempting to be more ambitious and try flowers. These are more difficult than bottles and jars, but you can bluff your way through by giving impressions of flowers rather than portraits, using dabs of muted colour on a slightly moist paper. If you are anxious to do justice to the flowers, look at them closely; what might at first glance appear to be a colour change may turn out on closer examination to be the shadow of one petal on another, so you do not modify the colour you are using, but add a slightly darker colour to the wash or try taking off part of the wash with a damp brush. It is sometimes worthwhile analysing certain flowers, seeing how a rose is in the form of a spiral, and how even a flower such as a pansy is not merely a symmetrical group of petals around a centre. The spontaneous approach really does pay off in flower pictures; if you do flower paintings too tightly you are in unwitting competition with the professional botanical artists, and you (and most professional painters) will soon realize your shortcomings. Roughing in flowers with a pencil can often be more of a hindrance than a help; you may well find yourself running out of space when you have miscalculated the distance between bloom A and bloom B, while if you are drawing with the point of a brush or just putting in blotches of likely colour you amend and adjust as you go along. You can let the flower colours run into each other, but it can be very tiresome if the greens infiltrate the rose pinks, or snapdragon yellows.

In flower arrangements some of the leaves will be in deep shadow, and it is often a good idea to emphasize these shadowed leaves, even exaggerating them, so that the main flower colours stand out. The actual painting of a flower group can be carried out either light-to-dark or dark-to-light.

A lovely landscape of the English countryside. To convey the distance involved, the artist has used progressively stronger washes, from barely any colour at all on the horizon, to almost undiluted paint in the foreground.

The stages in making a
stencil. The stencil can be as
simple or as elaborate as
one wishes. The cutting-out
process is unquestionably
the most crucial and must
never be rushed.

Right: Tracing the image
onto the polythene.

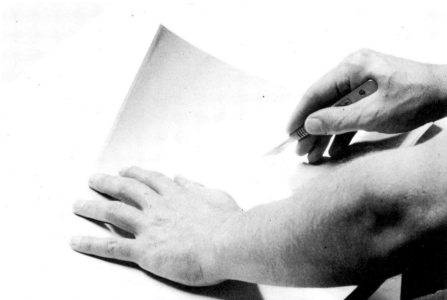

Cutting out the stencil.

Applying the wash.

Flower paintings are a good introduction to indoor scenes. These do not have to have every item picked out as if for an auctioneer's catalogue, and, as mentioned in the chapter on oil painting, you can keep some objects in mysterious shadow. It is an interesting process, working out how much you can suggest with a square of colour or a couple of verticals. For those who regard their paintings as a visual diary there is something uniquely satisfying in having a portrait of the interior of a well-loved room, and although interiors do pose a challenge it is one well worth taking up.

Many of the characteristics associated with interiors are shared by life paintings, in particular getting the perspective and the foreshortening right. It is vital to get the eye level set in accurately, and as you will have objects which straddle the eye level you will have parts of this object appearing to go up and others down. The vanishing points of the boundary line between walls and ceiling should be worked out; they will rarely fall within the scope of the picture. The same goes for the division between walls and floors. You will probably not get floor area and ceiling area in together, but even so it is useful to know what their vanishing points are. Getting these right will establish the correct dimensions of the room. There is no need to accentuate the wall/ceiling wall/floor dividing line heavily as a preliminary step. Roughly sketching it in is sufficient.

It is often more satisfactory to paint direct without pencil outlines, using the point of the brush to establish where things are and getting the tones in, leaving any detail to a later stage. It is easier if there is just one light source, either a window or a light. With a standard lamp or table lamp you can establish where you want your light source – in other words you can pose your interior to suit yourself.

As with still life and flower arrangements, one advantage of the interior is that it does not move around, and you can spend as much time on it as you like – if you are not using natural light from a window, which of course will mean that the shadows are constantly altering. In doing interiors, you can explore to the full the possibilities of direct painting, and as you become more adept you can create more difficult problems, for example using additional light sources or putting in a mirror.

If you are painting direct and are aiming for effect rather than an inventory, use a rough paper where detail is difficult to put down. With rough paper it is important to dampen it first, for otherwise you will find that the paint is adhering to only part of the surface. This creates a sparkling effect as there is a good deal of paper exposed, and if you want this by all means leave the paper dry.

If you go to an exhibition of amateur artists you will find very few interiors. They *are* more difficult than the ordinary open-air landscape, but they can be no less satisfying. You may find that you have a high ratio of failures in painting direct without pencil guide-lines. If you are in a sketching club and painting outdoors you may not want

these failures exposed, while if you are painting interiors you can happily discard them (or wash them off and start again on the same sheet of paper, maybe leaving the vestiges of the previous attempt to show you where you went wrong).

Watercolours are usually one-offs, but there may be occasions where you want repeats, perhaps for personalized Christmas cards. There is no way you can repeat a watercolour *exactly*, but you can get a close approximation by using homemade stencils. It is easy to make a stencil. The best kind of material is fairly thick polythene of the type used to make office folders or envelopes. Trace the subject with tracing-paper, and then place carbon paper between the tracing-paper and the polythene. You then go over the tracing with a ball-point pen or a hard pencil of at least 2H grade. Do not use subjects with interior spaces, as these pieces will drop out when you cut out your stencil. You can use either the cut-out part, or the empty space from which the cut-out comes.

To cut out the stencil you need a pair of small scissors or a scalpel (available from good art shops, and more suitable than craft knives as they are smaller). You can prepare the paper with a wash if you wish, wait for it to dry *thoroughly*, and then, firmly holding the stencil down on the paper, go *over* the polythene with your second wash so that the paint outlines your subject. This is when you are using the actual cut-out. If you are using the polythene from which the cut-out has been extracted, you will lay your wash over the space and over the adjacent area of stencil. Take care in lifting the stencil up, preferably leaving it there until the wash has dried. You should find that you have your design just as you traced it in.

There are many different ways you can use stencils. You can overlap the washes, you can add pure colour to the wash design, and, by not applying a first all-over wash, you can draw the subject in masking fluid. If you do this you can take off the stencil when the fluid has dried (not long) and apply an all-over wash to the paper. When this wash has thoroughly dried, you can peel off the masking fluid, and thus you have a white design to which you can do what you like. A smooth paper is preferable to rough when using stencils.

Stencils can be very intricate, and it is well worth spending time on the cutting-out process. If you enjoy experimenting, the use of stencils can be very stimulating. Overlapping stencils can create new shapes to fire the imagination.

GOUACHE

It is not a difficult transition from orthodox watercolour to gouache, and you can use the same equipment, plus bristle brushes and a palette knife. There is no need to change brushes if you are employing both gouache and watercolour in the same picture, and indeed gouache diluted is not far removed from ordinary watercolour, though perhaps a little grainier. You can use gouache by

Watercolour is used here much more strongly than in previous examples. Almost pure colour, applied with a small brush, is used for all the line detail in the foreground.

Winter scenes containing snow can be something of a challenge, and it often helps to counteract the sheer white of the snow with off white.

Far right: An impressionistic watercolour study. There were seven stages in its genesis: (1) a charcoal sketch; (2) a wash of Payne's grey and ultramarine for the sky, the clouds being taken out with blotting paper; (3) the first shadows were added to the land-based objects, in Payne's grey and raw umber; (4) the sea was put in with washes of viridian with blue and raw umber, much diluted, blending in with an orange wash which became the sandy foreground. Payne's grey was added at the foot of the picture. The orange and grey washes were allowed to overlap the shadows; (5) the local colour was put in with crimson, burnt sienna, and yellow ochre, and some detail was added; (6) the shadows were reinforced, and the horizon was affirmed with ultramarine; (7) the picture was tidied up (but not too much so), and the outlines of the objects were strengthened with Vandyke brown. Foreground detail was applied in burnt sienna, yellow ochre, and Payne's grey. Throughout the painting process, no colour was used at anything like full strength. The paper used was a heavyweight watercolour paper, slightly rough and therefore discouraging pettyfogging detail. Two soft brushes were used, a half-inch flat, and a medium (number three) pointed.

Below: A wartime 'home front' scene carried out in a series of self-contained flat washes in a colour scheme restricted to browns and greens. There was no improvisation in this watercolour, and the whole was laid down in pencil, with the exception of the sky. The whites everywhere are the whites of the paper showing through, and some of the textures are produced by rubbing off the wash with an eraser, which gives a pleasant mottled result (useful for mist effects).

Gouache is an ideal medium for applying areas of flat colour. In this street scene, basic areas of flat colour have been painted and then pen and ink work has been added, giving the painting an 'illustrative' effect.

Golden Yellow

Crimson

Burnt Sienna

Violet

Cobalt Blue

Permanent Green

White

Black

This picture, painted in gouache, shows that a still life need not necessarily be made up of exotic fruit and flowers. Anything in the home, such as these jam tarts, can become the subject of your painting.

itself, or in association with any of the water-based mediums. It is perfect for fine and 'hard line' work, though if it is used thickly there *is* a tendency for subsequent detail to 'float' on top.

Gouache dries lighter than when first applied, but this affects mainly the pastel tints, and the blacks and dark colours are very solid when used at full strength. The caps of gouache tubes should always be kept on otherwise the paint will dry out; it dries out far more rapidly than the pigment in watercolour tubes. An absolutely solid tube of paint can be annoying, but it *can* be used by scraping out the paint and putting it in the depressions of a palette. You will never be able to recapture the full density of the stronger colours, but it will remain workable.

Watercolour paper takes gouache very well indeed, but mounting board and card are also excellent surfaces, as gouache does not need a tooth and if a smooth effect is wanted there is no better medium. Gouache in pans is not nearly so pleasant to use. Gouache is *not* such a powerful covering agent as acrylic, and for quick successive thick coats of paint acrylic is better. If you are using a thick creamy mix of gouache always start with enough, because its tendency to dry out lighter makes it very difficult to repeat the exact colour when mixing up a fresh quantity. For an all-over absolutely even matt surface, gouache is supreme, and it is ideal for decorative purposes, having the virtues of the old-fashioned medium of tempera without the somewhat bizarre preparations (tempera uses raw egg). Gouache is a refined form of distemper, and for very large areas some artists use distemper and its various modern offshoots.

As a preliminary exercise, the sea scene mentioned above and in the chapter on oil painting is an ideal starting-off point. Put in all the components firmly in pencil, and fill in the areas with flat colour, ignoring light and shade, and making a pattern of the subject. You can use a large flat soft brush of sable or nylon for the larger areas, a smaller flat one for the boat and the land, and make certain that there is no overlap of colour by drawing the brush sideways along the outlines. If there is a mast on the ship this can be put in with a small sable. To get a really crisp horizon, lay a strip of masking tape along the horizon line and apply the paint so that it overlaps the tape. If you do a still-life study in gouache you can begin by laying a wash of much diluted gouache over the entire paper surface, rough in your design (better at this stage as diluted gouache is a better covering agent than watercolour), and build up, gradually reducing the amount of water in your mix so that at the end you are using the gouache straight from the tube. Do not leave paper peeping through for your highlights, but use white paint.

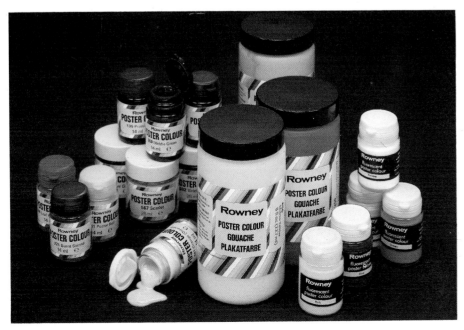

A selection of gouache and poster paints, available from most art shops.

CHAPTER 4

ACRYLICS

WHAT ARE ACRYLICS?

Acrylics are the only new paint to have come onto the market for centuries. Introduced to Britain in 1962, they are as versatile as it is possible to imagine. They can be used thickly like oil paints, or in transparent washes like watercolours. They can be applied to almost any surface whether it be paper, panel, cardboard or canvas. Their main attribute is that they dry *very* quickly and are ideal for those who work at top speed and like to see a finished picture in half an hour. They dry too quickly for some, but the drying speed can be slowed down with a retarder, and there are all kinds of additives such as mediums and texture pastes to suit every taste, though normally water is used as the painting agent. Van Gogh would have loved acrylics. Some established painters are suspicious of them despite their many claims (justified). If there is one thing they lack, it is subtlety. They are truly a product of the technological age, as efficient as a video recorder.

WHAT MATERIALS ARE NEEDED?

Paints These come in fairly large tubes, as acrylic paint is often used in bulk, and there is a very large range. Because acrylic dries very rapidly the top should always be kept on.

Mediums and Glosses These can be used at will, and impart a lustrous texture. Used with water acrylic is slightly matt.

Retarder This slows down the drying process, but never to the same extent as one normally gets with oil paints. To dedicated users of acrylic the adding of a retarder defeats what to many is the medium's great asset – rapid drying and the consequent ability to apply coat after coat within a few minutes. Acrylic paint is opaque when used thickly, and obliterates what has gone before, except when diluted and used as a glaze.

Texture Paste An optional extra, as you can build up texture anyway, and using thick pigment you can get what textures you want.

Primer This is a thick white paint rather like household undercoat and is used to paint on an absorbent surface, though size is better (and cheaper).

Varnish Acrylic varnish is a curious milky substance, and when used has the effect of completely obliterating the picture surface until it starts drying, when it is quite transparent. There is no reason why the traditional varnishes as used in oil painting cannot be used.

Brushes Nylon brushes *only* should be used. More people have discarded acrylic because of clogged brushes than for any other reason. Acrylic paint dries not only on the picture, but on the brushes, and only methylated spirits will clean them and only then if caught in time. The remedy is simple. *Always* keep the brushes in water, *not* point down but fairly flat in a brush tray. Nylon brushes will last for years if this practice is adopted. Do not be put off by nylon brushes; they are superb, even the smallest ones marked 00. If you really want a rough paint texture, you can use bristle, but the same advice applies – always keep them in water. Some artists still prefer to use sable for fine work, but these will suffer if kept in water continuously. Use the complete range of brush sizes from very large to very small.

Palette Knives Palette knives come in several sizes, and are useful in acrylics. Do not let the paint dry on the steel of the knife, for although it can be scraped off there is always a danger of damaging the thin steel of the smaller palette knives. Acrylic is ideally suited to palette-knife work, as it is not messy and does not ooze oil all over the place.

Palettes and Mixing Trays There is something on the market called a Staywet Palette, perfect for acrylics for as the name implies it stays wet and stops the paint coagulating. It is worth noting that the bigger a blob of paint in the tray or on an ordinary palette the longer it will take to dry out. In normal use, acrylic paint will *not* dry out on the palette before it can be used, and if in doubt add water to keep it moist. When acrylic paints start to dry on the palette, a crust forms. The paint can still be used if this crust is prised off with the tip of a palette knife.

Paper Almost any type can be used, but cartridge paper is as good as anything, and for those who like to use their paint smooth mounting board or white card is suitable. If you are using acrylic paint fairly thickly, watercolour paper is rather an expensive option. Because of the heaviness of the paint, thin paper is not really advisable. Canvas is excellent, but no better than card unless you are keen on using the natural texture of the canvas without overlaying it with too much paint.

Easel Acrylic lends itself to broad handling, and consequently an easel is essential if you like a bold style with lots of bravura and not too much detail.

Pencils and Charcoal Because of the great covering ability of acrylic, any medium you use to lay down your design will be obliterated by the paint (unless you are using it in thin watercolour style). If you are painting in several layers, making use of acrylic's drying rapidity, remember that you may need something to apply a design or an outline on to the *earlier* layers. In this event, bear in mind pastels or a felt-pen, something that will carry a line over paint ridges better than pencil.

Water Containers No less than three, one for clean water, one for less clean water, and one to splash the brushes around in between changes of colour. The brush tray *should* hold the brushes not at that moment being used, but if you are working at top speed it is more convenient to pop the brushes into the medium-clean water and trust that the points won't be damaged (nylon is very resilient and there is not much risk).

Masking Tape A very useful material, suitable for fixing paper to a drawing-board instead of draw-ing-pins, and also of great help in painting straight edges (the tape is laid alongside the area to be covered, and is then taken up when the paint has been applied, taking with it the ragged edge of paint and leaving an absolute straight edge). For irregular areas, including circles, the masking tape can be stuck around the area to be covered. Of course, as masking tape comes in rolls of vary-ing thickness, the tape will be buckled, but that does not matter.

Drawing-Board As always, this is an optional extra depending on what you are painting on (techni-cally known as the ground), but essential if you are using an easel and paper.

In addition you will add all kinds of odds and ends to your working material from time to time, and do not be afraid to improvise. A pair of dividers may come in useful if you want to compare one line or area of paintwork with another or to calculate distances between point A and point B. You may

find that you want to 'work up' your textures, and that the usual range of brushes do not give quite the effect you want. Two handy stand-bys are old toothbrushes and old shaving brushes, which give a texture of their own, unrepeatable with ordinary custom-made paint brushes. You can achieve interesting textures in acrylic by scoring the paint surface while still wet, and the point of a pair of dividers will do this, as will a knitting-needle or one of the blades of a pair of scissors.

HOW DO I START?

As always, get something down before you get transfixed by the blank paper, but if you are ex-ceptionally modest and feel that blank paper is wasted on you get something down on a sheet of newspaper or some old wrapping paper. Acrylic is an ideal medium for newcomers to painting, be-cause whatever you put down can almost im-mediately be obliterated by more paint.

You may like to get the feel of acrylics, and work out for yourself how much water you need on the brush, whether you prefer to use a medium with the paint rather than water, and how the paint goes down compared with other sorts of paint you have used. You can do this whether making a picture or merely doodling; making some kind of picture is certainly more interesting.

When you take up acrylic, you may not want to do it with an audience, so you will not want to try

In this abstract painting of trees, acrylic has been densely applied rather like oil paint.

Painting wood is often a stumbling block for artists. Rather than trying to paint every individual grain and knot (rather like leaves), a general impression of the wood is preferable. Here the artist has painted the basic flat colour and gradually added a 'feel' of the detail.

Raw Sienna

Burnt Sienna

Deep Brilliant Red

Titanium White

Raw Umber and Light Red

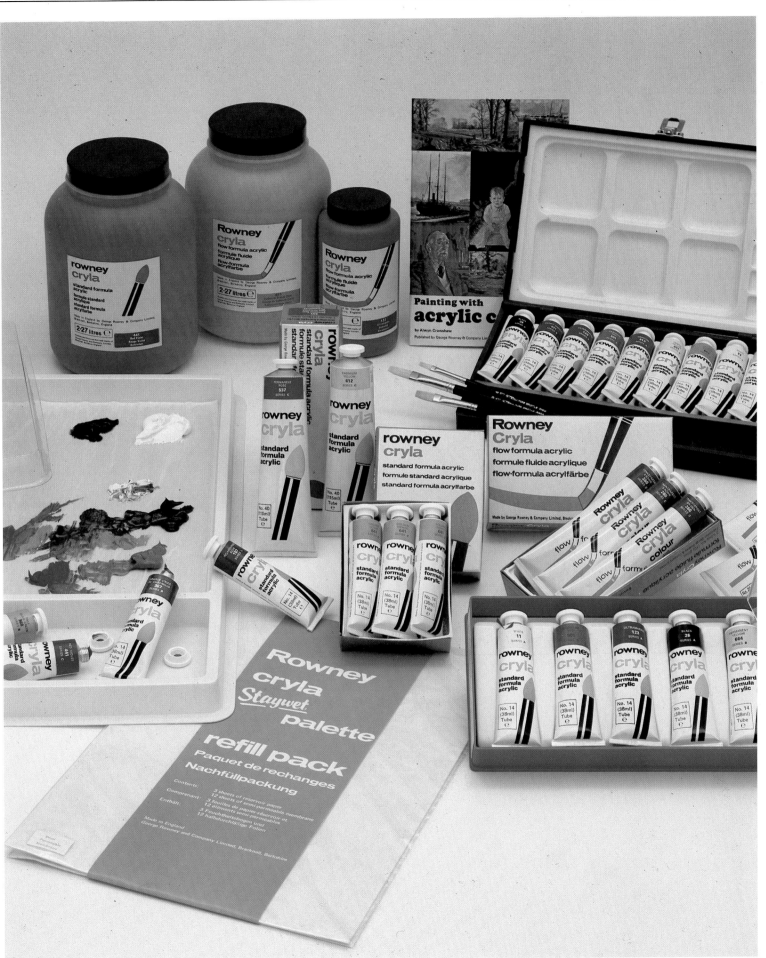

Materials available for acrylic painting.

Acrylic paint can be handled like oil paint – provided you are quick! In this painting of a deserted beach, the paint has been applied totally by palette knife.

In this painting of a Spanish
sunset the artist, rather than
trying to re-create the
original photograph, has
chosen to simplify the
shapes and colours, while
still retaining the heat and
atmosphere.

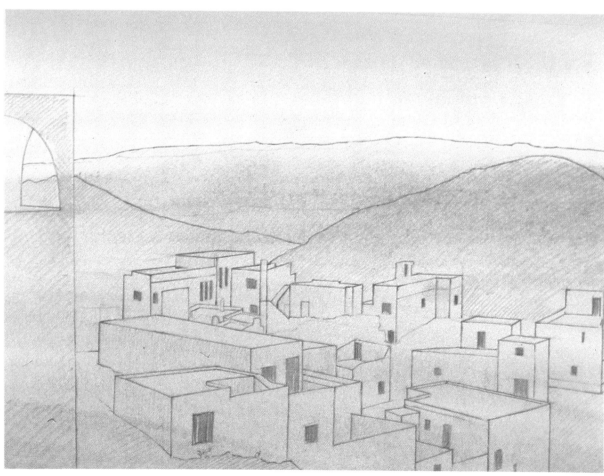

Medium Yellow

Yellow Orange

Orange Red

Medium Magenta

Prism Violet

Burnt Sienna

Titanium White

Black

it out in a life class or outdoors. If you are indoors, perhaps a still life, either imaginary or created from the objects near at hand – a loaf of bread, some fruit, maybe a jug. You can draw these in pencil fairly roughly, just sufficient to place the shapes on your working surface, and then put in your patches of colour. If you are not as yet too certain about your handling of colour, use a few colours, or perhaps just black and white, which gives you all the tone you want. Get the shapes more or less right, and then put in the edges as loosely or tightly as you wish. Try and make the picture hang together, and try not to make it too bright. Sometimes it is an effort to keep the painting low in tone (lower than it is in real life), but muddy colours have their own appeal and in the 1950s and 1960s they were the favourites among contemporary artists of the new realist school.

Perhaps you would prefer to kick off with a landscape, either imaginary or sparked off by a photograph or one of your own drawings. If you have already tried watercolour and have found that you can get along with it, do a watercolour first, and use acrylic on top of that. Or use watercolour washes to put in the feel of a landscape without being precise, and then build upon this, using transparent acrylic washes as if you were continuing to paint in watercolour. Then you may, or may not, use opaque acrylic on top of that.

There is no *best* way, in any medium, to paint a picture; there are *convenient* ways, there are ways that suit you and you alone, and to find out whether acrylic is a medium you want to persist with – after spending the money to buy the equipment and materials – you want to be *aware* of the techniques, even if you do not use them. Many of the techniques associated with acrylic painting have been lifted from oil-painting methods. One of these is the 'wet on wet' technique, which means exactly what it says, applying wet paint on to wet paint, which helps to merge colours, and is very useful for skies. You can use the acrylic very wet, or you can add retarder. The reverse of transparent acrylic paint is the use of texture paste. You may wish to build up areas of pigment so that the painting is almost like a relief, and the effect can be quite impressive, especially in the foreground of a picture. Being white, texture paste when mixed with paint tends to weaken the colour, and if you want darks it is best to lay down the texture paste first and add the dark colour when the texture paste is dry.

When the surface of the ground is porous, such as an untreated canvas, acrylic paint can be used thinly as a stain, but for general purposes this has only a limited appeal. In the first instance, you will probably want to use the full body of acrylic, either rough finish or smooth. When this surface is dry, there are a number of subsequent techniques to use. You can scumble, meaning drawing a dry brush loaded with paint across the dry surface, so that some adheres and some does not. It is no good trying to do fine work using this technique, but it adds texture to a painting and is good for doing water ripples. Scumbling using a dry

Far left: In this three-stage painting of a churchyard, acrylic has been used almost as watercolour, again showing the versatility of the medium.

Left: An acrylic study of a nude, showing the freedom of brushwork possible in this medium. Note the use of scumble.

brush and very little paint is ideal for mist and fog effects, and also to obscure partially a distant scene which may have become too prominent.

Another worthwhile technique is glazing, which is putting a transparent or semi-transparent wash over the existing picture. The colour should be heavily diluted with water or medium (which will make the glaze more shiny) and it is perhaps best applied with a soft brush, whereas scumbling is most effectively done with bristle or nylon. There is no limit to the number of glazes you can apply, and by a shrewd medley of glazes you can alter the whole character of a picture. You can experiment with taking some of the glaze out of certain areas using a piece of rag, and you must not think that glazes are necessarily light in colour. There is no reason, for dramatic effect, why black should not be used as a glazing colour.

When you are putting on a glaze or using acrylics in a diluted form do not expect quite the same feel as using watercolour wash. As I have said, acrylic is not a subtle medium, and do not expect the same kind of effect. Be prepared for a little annoyance when the colour dries out more quickly than you had anticipated. However, this is more than compensated by its covering properties; you can put white on black and confidently predict that the black will not show through.

Cobalt Blue

Permanent Green Deep

Burnt Sienna

Yellow Orange

Raw Sienna

Ivory Black

Titanium White

Acrylic can be used as a very dense medium, with good covering power. Notice how the preliminary outline, taken from a drawing, is totally covered by the final painting. Much detail, including shading, can be drawn and painted over, without fear of show-through.

This painting conveys
the blustery and eerie
atmosphere of a country
lane.

CHAPTER 5

PASTELS

WHAT ARE PASTELS?

Pastels are powdered colours mixed with water and chalk or oil and chalk, and made into sticks. Some manufacturers put in a binder to stop the pastels crumbling; the softer the pastel, the less binding is used. Water-based pastels are more often used than oil pastels.

WHAT MATERIALS ARE NEEDED?

A selection of pastels Pastels are sold in boxes, with a compartment for each pastel, and to stop the sticks rattling about they are protected by a layer of cotton-wool or tissue. There are several hundred tints available, but there are 'basic' boxes of 12 or 16, and this selection can be added to at will as pastels are also sold separately. The softer water-based pastels are the most useful.

Paper The most popular kind of paper is called Ingres, and it comes in various sizes and colours. It has a slight tooth, which is ideal for picking up the pastel powder. Any kind of paper can be used, such as watercolour paper, brown wrapping paper, cartridge paper, cardboard, and even sandpaper.

A Drawing Board Although not absolutely essential, a drawing board is very useful, as the paper can be fixed to it with drawing-pins or Scotch tape (or masking tape). Some artists prefer to work on a surface which has more 'give'; in which case, a pad of folded newspaper is placed under the pastel paper.

An easel Again, this is a matter of choice. Some artists prefer to work on a flat surface, but when using an easel the surplus pastel powder falls off and makes the surface less messy.

Charcoal Charcoal comes in thin sticks, and is very useful to sketch out the preliminary design. Charcoal does not have any real bite, and does not overwhelm the pastel. It also mixes very well with pastel, and can be taken out with an eraser or even the finger tip.

Pencils Pencils can be used to make preliminary sketches, and a softer rather than a harder pencil is better (2B or 4B though some prefer HB, which is neither hard nor soft and is the ordinary office pencil). Pencil in general should not be used in the final stages of a pastel picture, as it shows up shiny.

Pastel Pencils Pastel pencils are quite new, and are merely pastels in the form of a pencil, useful for fine work, but rather tiresome as the wood has to be constantly shaved away.

Stumps or Torchons These are compressed 'pencils'
of blotting-paper or a similar substance, used for blending the pastel colours on the paper.

Tissues Tissues can also be used to blend the pastel colours on the paper, but they are useful to have about as in using pastels the hands tend to get powdery.

Cotton Buds Again these are very suitable for blending pastel colours, especially for fine work. They can also be used to apply pastel powder where the pastel itself is too clumsy.

Erasers The best kind of erasers are putty rubbers; ordinary pencil erasers are too harsh, and can mess up the tooth of the paper. The use of any kind of eraser should be kept to a minimum, except for preliminary sketches. When pastels are applied layer on layer, an eraser can ruin the whole thing.

Fixative Some artists prefer not to use a fixative, as they think it takes some of the freshness away, but the risks of smudging a pastel picture are great enough to make a fixative very useful. Fixatives are sold in liquid form, and used with a mouth-spray (two narrow metal tubes on a hinge, and used with the tubes at right angles), or in aerosol cans (more convenient). Full instructions go with the cans. When the fixative is used, the pastel picture goes very dark, which can be alarming the first time, but it dries out in a few minutes, without any great colour change taking place.

Vigorous studies in the use of pastel.

The immense variety of
pastels and accessories.

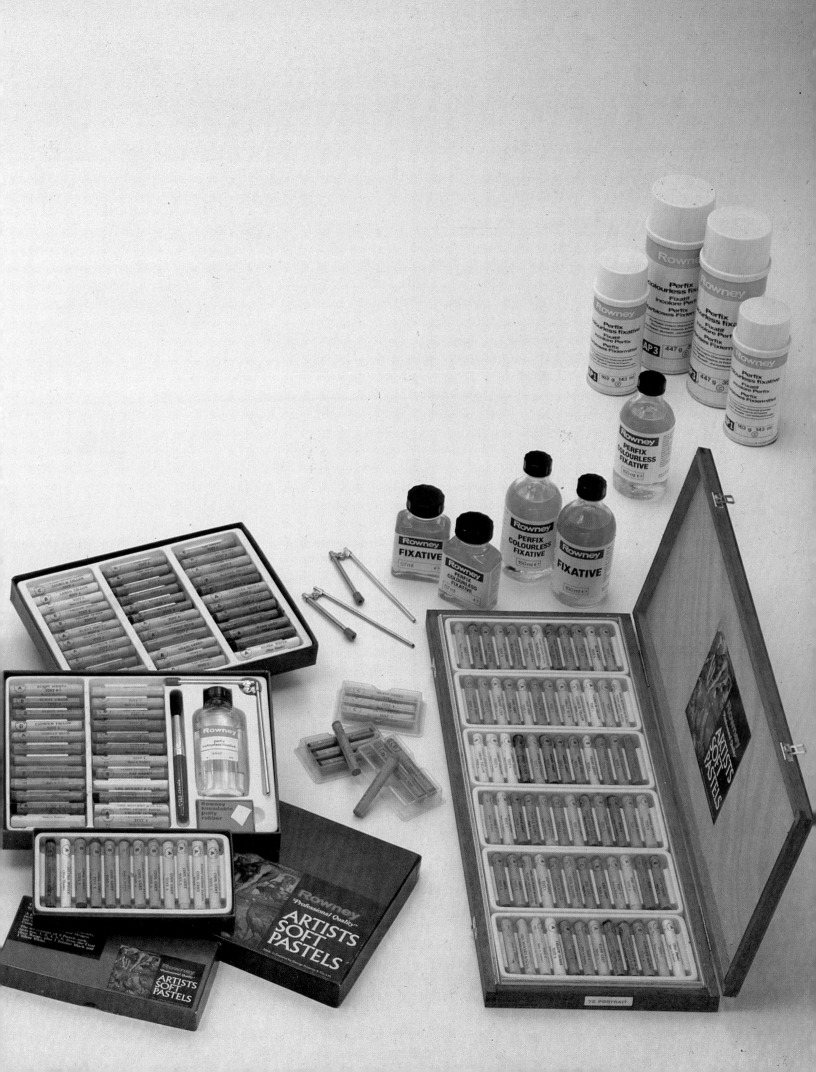

Brushes Both soft and bristle brushes can be used in association with pastel, to blend the dry pastel, or used with water to turn the powder into a paste (the word pastel comes from the word paste). This paste can be drawn over with dry pastel. Bristle brushes can impart interesting textures to the picture surface. Some artists do not use brushes at all, and it is entirely up to you.

This is the basic equipment for painting in pastels, but there are extras which you can add at will. If you wish to do a detailed underpainting on which you will put your pastels later, you may want to do this in watercolour, acrylic, pen and ink, or felt pen. All these go well with pastels, simply because they go with water. The thing is to experiment, to find out what suits you. It may be that the sight of a clean sheet of paper is daunting. In which case, get something down on it right away, anything, even a splash of colour by using a sponge (which can spark off an idea for a picture, just as looking at a fire).

HOW DO I START?

One of the most exciting things about pastels is that the artist can exercise ingenuity to the full, and there are absolutely no rules. Some people prefer to start their painting with only the haziest idea of what it is to be about, while others prefer a detailed drawing. These drawings can be outline drawings only, or they can be finished drawings in their own right, with colour, and light and shade. The pastels can then be used to fill in the colour.

Before putting pastel to paper, it is worthwhile going through the various subjects of paintings, in descending order of suitability for pastel: Portrait and Figure, Still Life, Nature, Landscape, Abstract. Naturally all these subjects *can* be done with pastel. The kind of picture you are going to do in some way or other is bound to influence the kind of technique you are going to employ. Another important factor is whether you are doing a picture from life, with the subject before you, doing a picture from a photograph, postcard, or other illustration, or if you are doing a picture from imagination. Illustrations are often a good taking-off point, stimulating a memory, or suggesting a line of approach. There is something to be said for trying to copy a famous pastel painting from a colour photograph.

The Very First Steps
Decide what kind of paper you are going to use, pin it or Scotch-tape it to a drawing board, or place it on a flat surface, with or without a pad of newspaper beneath the paper. Place your materials within easy reach – if you are right-handed keep the pastels by the right of the paper. It may seem obvious, but sometimes the obvious is overlooked. When the pastels are new, they have neat labels on transparent wraps; these labels soon go as the pastels become used, so it is no bad idea to keep the pastels on a labelled tray – a piece of corrugated

The building-up of a head, using pastels. Here, the artist has worked from a sketchy outline through to a very finished study.

paper is ideal. The sticks of pastel soon break any way, so if it is more convenient break them before-hand into one-inch lengths. Pastels being used will soon get dusty, with specks of other colours adhering to them, but there are ways to clean them off as soon as they have done their job.

Beginning the Picture
The first marks do not have to be important. As suggested earlier, you can give the paper a few splashes of colour with a sponge or perhaps a soft brush. You may care to develop this in water-colour if the first signs are promising. If you have a definite object before you, then you may wish to put down your first impressions in charcoal, which rubs out easily with an eraser or the finger-tip. Charcoal can be held like a pencil, or loosely by the far end. Do not press too hard on it as it will snap.

If you are painting with a subject in front of you, the still life can be most satisfying. Ordinary

kitchen equipment is a good starter, maybe com-bined with a loaf of bread and some china. There is nothing better than an assortment of fruit as a still-life subject – far easier to paint in any me-dium than flowers.

There is always a temptation to draw in outline, but remember that a line does not exist in nature – it is merely the edge of a shape. So if you can think in shapes rather than outlines it is a big ad-vance; and shapes are easier to do than outlines. Of course, you need to define the edges of the shapes, but a good way to get the shape down is to use the *side* of a piece of charcoal, so you are work-ing with a flat piece.

These first marks can be tentative, as you try to get the feel of it. They can be squiggles, they can be lines exploring the way the shapes go, they can be little blotches setting down the shadows. No matter what medium you are working in, remem-ber that light and shade are vitally important, far more important than colour in making a picture

In this still life, the artist has chosen very brightly coloured objects with a bright background. He has used an outline, rather than the suggestion of shadow for shape, and has finger-blended the pastels.

which is 'like'. It is a good idea when setting up a still life (or for that matter when doing a figure painting or a portrait) to have strong light coming in from one source (easier from the sides, more difficult from the front, more difficult still from the back). Light and shade *define* the forms or shapes.

It cannot be stressed too often that the way you work is determined by you and you alone. If you feel that you want to put in the outlines first, and fill in from there, go ahead.

Your preliminary sketches may seem meaningless to everyone except you, but you may know exactly what is going to come out. The main object

should be to get the articles you are painting coming together on the paper as a coherent group, not odd things scattered around by themselves. This is more important than accuracy; no one is going to award you a prize if the bump on an apple is absolutely right or if the curve of a banana is too pronounced. Unless your aim is to be purely decor-

ative, try to get the feeling of the solidity of the objects you are painting. You do this simply by finding out where the light is falling, and darkening those areas which are shadowed.

There are two kinds of shadows. There is the shadow which occurs away from the light, and there is the cast shadow, in which an object

Applying the Pastel

The natural way to use pastel is to hold the stick like a pencil and using the end to colour the paper. Held at a slant, the pastel will give a thin line; held upright, a thicker line. Held lightly, the pastel will deposit less colour on the paper, and the colour of the paper will show through. Sometimes the colour of the paper can be the background without anything more needing to be done to it.

There are numerous ways to apply the pastel. Short stabs of colour can be put down, giving a patchwork effect. Various colours can be set side by side in thin strips, or 'cross-hatching' can be used – making a network of strokes, like a crossword, either the same colour or different colours. Dots of colour can be used, or areas of colour can be laid down by using the pastel on its side, applied thickly by pressing down, or thinly by a lighter touch. All these techniques can be combined.

It is much better to experiment with all these methods when painting a picture than as meaningless exercises on a piece of paper. A picture of some sort is bound to emerge – it may not be up to much but in all art the painter gets better. A technique acquired is a permanent acquisition.

Unlike watercolours and oils, pastel colours are not mixed or blended beforehand but are mingled on the paper, using contrasting dots or patches of colour, cross-hatching, or, the favourite way and the one most used by the great pastel painters of the past, blending the colours together with the finger-tip, a stump or torchon, tissue, a cotton-bud, or a brush. Old-fashioned art-teachers frown on this finger-blending, as they say it destroys the 'bloom' of pastel.

What is this bloom? It is the effect arising from the reflection of light on the tiny granules of pigment. It can be destroyed by too much rubbing, but the remedy is to apply more pastel after the colours have been suitably blended. You have to use some discretion when finger-blending, for it is easy to make a muddy mess when too many colours merge together.

Finger-blending can produce a perfectly even colour surface, to which shading can be added by a few granules of darker colour. This does not have to be black. Sometimes a subtle shading is wanted, where the light area merges into a darker, as around an apple or orange. The colour can then be a darker tint of the same colour, or maybe a blue.

In the early stages of painting a pastel, the subject can be gently covered with a light single colour, to set the tone of the picture, and the shadows set out on this, with a touch of white to pick out the lightest parts. The 'real' colour can then be added. It is a matter of choice whether you do the picture bit by bit, or tackle the whole picture in stages, so that it all comes together at the end. If you think that the picture is becoming flat and boring, you can enliven the textures, either by using pastel in a different way or roughing up the surface with a dry bristle brush. The 'highlights', those vivid small patches of white which can make a picture live, should be reserved to the very end.

already in the shade throws a shadow over something else. Cast shadows are darker than ordinary shadows. Ignoring light and shade is the reason why so many amateurs' pictures in all mediums are flat, no matter how well they are coloured.

The preliminaries can naturally be done in pastel without the use of charcoal. It is best to use a neutral colour, though tempting to use black (neutral means a colour such as muted brown or grey). Black pastel is far more substantial a colour than charcoal, and not so easy to remove. Although pastels are opaque, some colours are more opaque than others. Again, however, it is a matter of personal choice, as you can build up a pastel picture layer upon layer until even the blackest underpainting is hidden. When you are using pastel for the preliminary sketch you can also use it on its side to give areas of colour rather than strokes.

Left and far left: The artist who made both these drawings, in oil pastel, has acquired his own technique of building up stages of colour and scratching through to reveal the layers. Both show a vigorous and adventurous use of the medium to create different moods.

Liberal use of pastel with
some blending, to produce a
lively picture of a seagull.

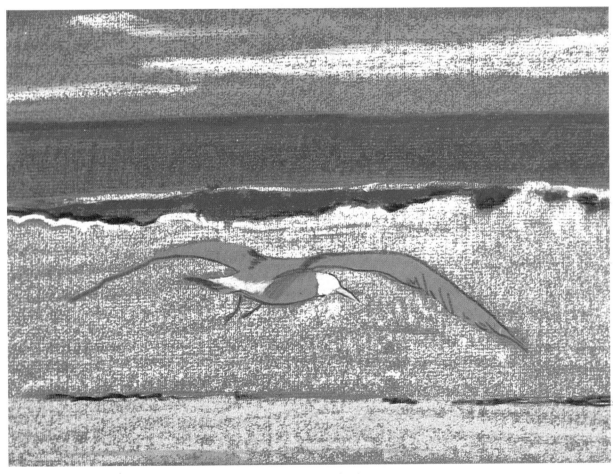

Far right: An oil pastel, again using a build-up of colours with blending and scratching to achieve several effects.

At some stage in a picture you will look at the blunt end of a worn-down pastel and wonder how you are going to get any kind of detail. This problem will occur particularly in portrait painting and landscape. Do you break off a short length of pastel so that you have another sharp edge? Do you grind the blunt end down with sandpaper? You can waste a lot of pastel, and in fact a stick of pastel is too clumsy, so that you have to resort to smaller fragments, too small to hold in the fingers. The answer is to hold a fragment of pastel with a pair of eyebrow tweezers, and use this to get fine detail, or make use of a pastel pencil. But do not expect pastels to give you the degree of precision you would get with watercolours or oils. Nor can you expect the kind of coverage you get from oils. On the other hand, it is very easy to be impressionistic or 'suggestive' with pastels, and once you are experienced it is the ideal medium for quick five-minute on-the-spot sketches – you can cover a sheet of paper in two seconds flat.

One of the great advantages of pastel is that correction can be carried out quickly and decisively, either by applying a further coat of pastel or by removing some, either with a putty rubber or the dry bristle brush. It is also easy to correct or transform tones, and alter any shapes, very important in portraiture where the proportions *must* be right. An excellent way to check accuracy is to hold a work-in-progress up to a mirror where any faults will stand out immediately. The speed with which you can work with pastel is a real asset when it comes to painting portraits; still life and landscape do not move. People, with the best will in the world, do.

There is always a temptation in pastel to make the colours too bright and, it must be said, insipid. If a picture is turning out tamely, a remedy is to mute *all* the pure colours with a neutral tint and add more colour very sparsely. If the greens of a landscape are too garish, blend in greys or some red. There is also a temptation to be satisfied with pastels that are over-bright; pastels can be rich and subdued, as the great masters of the 18th century have shown.

Closing Stages

Having reached the stage where the painting is coming along nicely, you should check that the picture hangs together well, and that the colour combination is right. The objects should look real and solid, and the light and shade realistic. The shadows should not be too harsh; if they are too black add in a lighter colour. If you want to focus attention on just one part of the picture (for example a face in a portrait) gently blur the edges of features you want to demote. If you want to highlight something add a fleck of white. If you consider the picture finished hold it upright and gently tap it on a table to get rid of surplus pastel dust. Then apply the fixative. Fixative can be applied at *any* stage throughout the painting, and pastel used on top. It is not a varnish.

Pastels are not usually varnished, though there is no reason why they should not be, provided that the paper is prepared beforehand by coating it with size. Untreated paper comes out in blotches if varnished. If you are going to varnish a pastel, the best ground to use is the kind of prepared canvas sold for oil painting. It goes without saying that varnish is *not* applied with a brush, but by means of an aerosol.

MOUNTING AND FRAMING PASTELS

Some people draw a margin round their paper before they start doing a pastel, and keep their picture inside this inner area. Others use what area of paper they want, and consequently the subject matter is not necessarily in the middle. A number of mounts should be kept handy, so that when the picture is completed a mount can be placed over it to see what needs to be in and what is superfluous.

Pastels can be framed like watercolours, with a cut cardboard mount to keep the picture surface off the glass. Large pastels tend to crinkle if mounted free, and should be pasted down on mounting board using wallpaper paste. The pastel is placed face down on a pad of newspaper, the back moistened with a large soft brush, and then put on one side while the mount is pasted. The pastel is then placed snug against the mounting board, making certain that there are no air pockets. Suitable mounts can be cut using a scalpel or craft knife.

Pastels can also be framed without using a cardboard mount, in which case a fillet of wood or card (known as a 'slip') is fitted round the edge of the inner frame so that it separates the pastel from the glass. Even after the use of fixative, a certain pastel-powder loss must be expected if the picture is directly against the glass. Pastels do not fade, nor are they subject to mould. If pastel pictures are stored they should be interleaved with tissue paper; there is a slight powder loss, but of no great consequence.

Oil Pastels

Oil pastels are less versatile than water-based pastels, and are really a substitute for painting in oils. They can be softened and applied to the surface with a palette knife, and, like ordinary oil paints, thinned with turpentine. No first-rate artist has bothered with oil pastels overmuch, and they are decidedly a second-best medium. Perhaps they are most useful as an oil-painting accessory, though some people might find that they take to them better than ordinary pastels, as they are denser in texture. They can be used on paper if they are employed in purely stick form, but if they are thinned with turpentine the paper will stain through, leaving the pastel surface dull. If paper is used, and the oil pastels are softened or diluted, it will need to be sized.

CHAPTER 6

FRAMING

Professional picture-framing can be an expensive business, and the prices vary enormously. One framer may charge £6, while another can do exactly the same job for £15, or even more. The most reasonable are those who do framing 'for the trade', as art shops which do framing as a side-line are inclined to be on the expensive side. It is much cheaper to do the framing yourself.

There are framing kits at reasonable prices, but the finished product rarely turns out as well as expected, and it is often better to use existing frames, bought at second-hand or junk shops for a pound or two. Open-air markets are a very good source of supply for second-hand frames, and even those in a damaged condition need not be scorned.

Basically there are two kinds of frames, those without glass for oil paintings and perhaps acrylic, and those with glass for most other types of picture. If you are interested in watercolours there is no point in buying up quantities of frames without glass, for a visit to a hardware store will convince you that glass is not cheap, and will often come to more than the cost of the frame.

In the old days picture frames for oil paintings were gilt and ornate, and nothing sets off oil paintings of the traditional type more than being set in a gilt frame. The mouldings of these are made out of gesso, which is really not much more than plaster of Paris, which has been gilded over. It is very unusual to pick up gilt frames at reasonable prices with all the moulding intact, but a bit of missing moulding, if it does not go through to the wood underneath, does not detract from the general look of the frame. Mouldings can be repaired by using modelling paste and then gilding over. There are various way to do this, but perhaps the easiest is by using Goldfinger, a proprietory substance in a tube which comes in different shades of gold and is applied by the finger or a soft cloth. The tubes are not cheap, but Goldfinger has an almost incredible covering capacity. For fine detail Goldfinger can be applied with a soft brush. Intricate mouldings in which sections project from the main body are kept in place by using wire, and the modelling paste adheres well to wire. The cheapest kind of wire by far is the green plastic coated wire sold in garden shops, which is flexible and strong.

Gesso is also used for more ordinary frames, applied quite thinly and then gilded or painted. Sometimes the damage to the gesso is considerable, but there is no need to despair of such frames for the gesso can be soaked off. It is better to immerse the frame in a tank of water and let it soak for a few days, whereupon the gesso can be eased off with a knife or a chisel. The wood used is often pine, and this can be painted or waxed, but make sure it is thoroughly dry before doing any finishing work.

Sometimes frames intended for oil paintings are found to be too large, and it is tempting to try to cut them down to the right size. There are various do-it-yourself gadgets available for cutting lengths of wood at 45° angles, but unless one is a skilled woodworker the results are rarely satisfactory,

for an error of a fraction of an inch throws the whole thing out and even the tiniest distortion in a frame looks odd. Even if the four sections for the frame turn out well it is not easy to nail or glue the pieces together.

If the frame turns out to be too small, it is worthwhile looking at the picture to see if it can be trimmed. Most painters instinctively leave a margin of inessential material, and nearly always some of this can be cropped. Naturally this cannot be done if the picture is on canvas, for any adjustment to the woodwork on which a canvas is stretched can be disastrous.

The great advantage of gilt frames and other frames intended for oil paintings is that they are deep, so as to accommodate the canvas on its stretcher, and if the frame is too shallow there will be a problem in getting the canvas to stay put, though the use of long panel pins, hammered in and then bent over the back of the canvas, can help.

Watercolours are usually mounted before being framed, and consequently the size of the frame is not too important. It is fashionable to frame small watercolours in large frames with a big area of mounting board. Mounting board is not expensive and comes in a variety of colours and tints, and the mounting board colour chosen can conveniently match the basic tone of the picture. One of the most useful colours is shiny gold, and this is one of the traditional mounting colours for watercolours. Watercolours in the traditional style always seem to look well set against gold.

Second-hand frames often contain mounts, but if they are foxed or dirty it is not worthwhile trying to refurbish them, and they are best thrown away. Cutting mounts is easy; all you need is a metal rule or straight-edge and a craft knife (though a scalpel, available from good art shops, is better still). There is only one disadvantage in making one's own mounts: it is difficult to get a bevelled edge, though there are mount-cutters on the market which do give a bevel. These are a blade set in a kind of miniature plane.

The first thing to do in mounting a picture is to decide exactly how much of the picture you want to use. It is often possible to dispense with a good section of sky and foreground in mounting landscapes to the advantage of the picture. Using a scalpel or a craft knife, cutting out the centre of the mount is not difficult. The main thing to watch out for is the position of the fingers holding the metal rule against the board. Do not try to cut the mounting board with one stroke – three or four strokes are much better. The intersecting pencil lines setting the dimensions of the picture space should not be too heavy, as when the piece of card has been cut out the lines should be rubbed out. A soft pencil about 4B should be used, or alternatively a pastel pencil, the lines of which brush off quite easily without the use of an eraser.

Second-hand frames, whether or not they already hold a picture, usually have vestiges of backing paper on the back of the existing mount, on the piece of wood which sometimes backs the picture, or on the backs of the frame. Often the wooden panel can be used again, but it is advisable to scrape off any odds and ends of backing paper, and it is essential to clear the back of the frame of loose ends. If not they have an uncanny habit of appearing on the glass just as you are closing up the picture. The glass, of course, should be thoroughly washed, and fly-specks scraped off. It is often difficult to see these until the picture is framed and in position, and when the glass is cleaned it should be put on a sheet of white paper and inspected for any obtrusive specks.

It is better to take out any existing tacks and not try to use them again. Glazing brads are the best for holding the glass, picture, and back-board in place, though professional framers use little slivers of flat metal. It is a matter of choice whether you fit a wooden panel, or a piece of card, on top of the mount. The main purpose of this is to hold the mount rigid and keep out dust. The backing-paper, which is usually ordinary brown paper glued to the edges of the frame and trimmed off with brown paper tape, also keeps out dust.

If the picture is equipped with a hanging cord, this should be discarded and replaced either with picture-hanging wire or plastic-coated garden wire. If the picture is very heavy, the wire should be used doubled over. Ring-screws (screws with eyelets) are better than hooks. Never use ordinary string as it dries out and breaks.

Left: Watercolours are usually framed with a simple wooden or metal frame and a broad mount or board surrounding the picture. Mounting boards are available in an immense variety of colours, enabling the artist to choose an appropriate board to enhance the painting.

Left: An ornate gilt frame is chosen to enhance this traditional oil painting.

Right: A selection of frames, showing the large variety available. You should choose a frame that enhances the painting and is also sympathetic to your decor.

Professional picture framers
at work.

CHAPTER 7

SELLING PAINTINGS

There are professional artists who make a very good living from their art, marine artists and portrait painters probably being the most successful, but there is absolutely no reason why you should not make money from your pictures. The first thing to remember is that artists living in attics who suddenly become famous overnight are the exception. Even if you are good it does not mean to say you will automatically make a lot of money at it, and with the present state of art criticism (bricks at the Tate Gallery and happenings masquerading as Art) who can say what is good? Except those who know what they like.

It is never a good thing to equate time spent painting a picture with the money received. This works both ways. In the heyday of American abstract-expressionism an artist could cover a canvas in 20 minutes and sell it for $10,000. Quite recently I saw a beautifully executed watercolour of roses which must have taken many hours to do, at least eight to 10. It was on sale in an art shop for £15. The artist was alive and well and living in the town, and obviously painting for money or otherwise why put the watercolour up for sale?

Perhaps it is being presumptuous to say that aggressively modern art is *not* saleable, unless you happen to be a known art personality (not necessarily an artist). This is not to decry modern or experimental art. Abstract and non-representational artists are usually backed by a gallery, who presumably guarantee the status of the artist.

There is nothing to stop you approaching one of the established London galleries to see if they would like to handle your work, but it is sensible to find out what sort of pictures they handle. *The Arts Review Yearbook and Directory*, published by Eaton House Publishers Ltd, 1 Whitehall Place, London SW1A 2HE, contains a comprehensive guide to London galleries and some provincial ones. It gives an indication of the type of pictures each gallery specializes in, though a visit to the galleries, most of which are in a fairly compact area of London, gives a better idea. Do *not* send original art work to a gallery, but only photographs, preferably transparencies, together with a covering letter addressed to the director, and a stamped addressed envelope. Commercial galleries charge a fairly high rate of commission of the order of 33 per cent, but they do all the advertising and promotion, and if you are accepted you become as it were one of their stable and are much to be envied.

It is often not realized that the annual Summer Exhibition at the Royal Academy is open to all. Anyone can submit up to three pictures, all of which go before a jury and are duly accepted or rejected. There is a small handling fee, and if a picture is accepted the Royal Academy charges commission at 20 per cent, plus VAT. The percentage of pictures accepted is quite small compared with the quantity sent in, so a rejection by the Royal Academy should not make you too downhearted. The process of judging is traditional, and acceptance or rejection depends very much on the likes and dislikes of the jury members. A refusal might merely mean that in this particular year everyone is sending in paintings of flowers, and enough is enough.

Complete details will be found in a leaflet of regulations called *Notice to artists* put out in mid-February each year, which is obtainable from the Royal Academy of Arts, Piccadilly, London W1C 0DS. The leaflet applies only to the exhibition held in the summer of the same year.

London galleries are not all in the magic square mile around Bond Street, and a look at the Yellow Pages in the telephone directory will reveal a plethora of galleries in most districts. Again, it is best to visit them, and the less pretentious galleries may be more suitable for your work than the prestigious ones in the West End. Their directors are more approachable and may well agree to look at your 'folio', the name given to a collection of drawings and paintings kept in a large folder. Obviously canvases cannot be included in a folio, and if they are large and cumbersome, transparencies are better as an introduction. These transparencies do not have to be more than adequate, and do not need to be taken by a professional photographer. Take your pictures into the garden on a sunny day, and put them on an easel or the back of a chair. Take two or three photographs of each painting, each with a different exposure time, and present the ones which came out best. It is a decided advantage to mount watercolours and drawings when building up a folio.

Provincial galleries can be a good deal less demanding than those in London, though the prices obtained can be considerably below those achieved in London. There is a greater market for scenes of local interest, and if you have a talent for landscapes and especially townscapes you have a very good chance of having some of your work taken on a commission basis, sale or return. If you are good at maritime pictures, it is sensible to approach galleries in towns with sea-going connections – yachting not ocean-going liners. A gallery in a seaport which has a marina has a marked advantage over one in Plymouth, for example.

If you live in a part of the world noted for natural beauty, there is a demand for local scenes in craft and gift shops, but only in the holiday season, and only if the owners feel that there is a ready market for your pictures. They have to make their living in a few months, and can ill-afford wall-space on possible and not probable sellers. In some beauty spots there are galleries on the spot. Some picturesque ports have a gallery right on the quayside, but you are competing with all the local artists, good, bad and indifferent, and a gallery owner in this situation may well be fully committed.

You naturally have an advantage if you know someone who has a shop, someone willing to show a few pictures. Fruit and vegetable shops may not be the first choice of a venue, but it is surprising how many general stores have the odd local painting on their walls or in a window. Some of these are so bad that the owner of the shop is really doing someone a favour.

The exterior of Waddington's, one of the many private art galleries in London.

The Royal Academy of Arts, in London. Anybody, whether amateur or professional, may submit work for possible selection and showing in the Academy's annual Summer Exhibition.

The Selection Committee for the Royal Academy Summer Exhibition, 1983. *Left to right:* Allen Jones, R.A., Robert Buhler, R.A., Roger de Grey, R.A., William Bowyer, R.A., H. Andrew Freeth, R.A., Peter Blake, R.A., and students of the Royal Academy School.

Nobody will buy your paintings if nobody sees them, and there is a middle way between modesty and aggressive self-publicizing. If you are thinking of selling your pictures try to make certain that they are worth selling. This can be difficult. A wife or husband may hide the truth from you, and you do need an outsider's opinion – not a friend for she or he may be, to say the least of it, guarded. If you like the look of the owner, ask an opinion at a commercial gallery. If you are a regular customer of an art shop, the owner will certainly be able to differentiate between a good painting and a bad one.

Again, a fellow artist who you realize is quite good would be a good choice as someone to ask an opinion of, but always be aware of the average person's wish to give the answer that is wanted. Sometimes you *will* have to ask a friend her or his opinion, and you will have to judge whether the reply is a fair one by reactions. If they break out in a cold sweat you have chosen the wrong person.

You must remember that a large number of people will not *know* whether you have done a good or bad painting. Their response may be based on the fact that they could not do it, and anything which is reasonably like the subject is acceptable. If you have a local antique shop, and, especially, if you are in the habit of going there and buying something, the owner may be an excellent person to approach for an opinion, provided that he is not being propositioned to put one of your pictures on his walls, though he may do this if he likes it well enough. Antique dealers come into contact with all kinds of art, and as they make a living assessing the market, their advice is worth having.

Friends may of course buy paintings from you, but this is no indication of their quality. They may merely be doing their duty. There is nothing more depressing than being gradually permitted to buy a painting which you honestly do not want.

Another option open to you, if you wish to exhibit, is the local art club or society. You may not have one, and if this is so, start one; you are then in the prime position to have pictures exhibited. In earlier chapters sketching clubs have been enthusiastically recommended, but there is a question mark against art societies, particularly if provincial and middle class. Art societies (or circles) have a tendency towards cliquishness and politicking, and although coffee-morning-type societies may welcome you into their bosoms it may be as a recruit rather than as an artist.

Exhibiting is a very different thing to selling, and it depends on your own ego whether you are happy to have a painting displayed where all can see it and know it is by you, but knowing that it only has a small chance of selling. If you do join an art society, do not be dismayed if a picture of inferior quality sells and yours does not. At village exhibitions, in which the only pictures which are excluded are saucy nudes, the purchase of a painting has nothing to do with quality.

Many of the professions have their own art societies, and as it is an axiom that those who are skilled in one facet of life are equally skilled at something else, many of the pictures shown at the exhibitions of these societies are of very high quality. Many large firms also encourage art societies formed from among their employees, and as working hours get less and leisure time more we can confidently predict a massive increase in such inexpensive patronage (cheaper than brass bands and not so rowdy as coach tours). No one would expect to make money from exhibitions of such extra-mural activities. Not that it matters. It may be agreeable to make money from painting, but no one would expect to make money from watching television, playing snap, or playing pool (unless you are a hustler, in which case you would probably not be reading this book!).

Far right: A group of portrait artists outside the National Portrait Gallery, London. They are popular with the many visitors to London and are often very skilled draughtsmen.

A private view at an art gallery.

GLOSSARY

acrylic paint
An oil-compatible synthetic medium which is
thinned out with water, linseed oil or turpentine.

advancing colours
Strong, warm or hot colours (red, orange or
yellow), usually unadulterated, which seem to
come to the surface of the picture.

aerial perspective: see *atmospheric perspective*

anamorphosis
The use of distortion to draw an object so that it
only appears normal when seen from an oblique
angle.

aquarelle
A painting made with transparent watercolour
washes.

atmospheric perspective
Creates the effect of distance by using less vivid
colours for distant objects, representing them as
they look in nature through light, air and
distance.

bleeding through
When underlayers of paint become visible
because the oil-based paints of the upper layers
have become transparent with time.

bloom
A film which develops on varnished surfaces and
in time almost obscures the picture.

body colours
Pigments which possess substance, as opposed to
transparent pigments.

brush drawing
A drawing made entirely with brush, usually in
a wash. This is a popular technique in Eastern
art.

caricature
A representation of a person or object which
exaggerates the characteristic features, usually
for humorous or satirical purposes.

cartoon
A preliminary full size drawing used as a model
for painting, mural, mosaic, tapestry, etc. It can
also be a caricature or an animated film made of
comic drawings.

casein paint
Alkaline casein-based paint produces effects
from transparency to thick textured opaqueness.

cera colla (Italian for wax glue)
An emulsion of wax and glue, which was used by
Byzantine artists for tempera painting.

chiaroscuro
The use of contrasting light and shade in
painting.

collage
A picture or design made from scraps of paper or
other everyday materials.

colour
Colour has the following attributes:

1 hue or tint: the actual colour.
2 intensity: the degree of purity, strength or
saturation.
3 value: the lightness or darkness of a colour,
the amount of light reflected or transmitted by
a coloured object.

colour perspective: see *atmospheric perspective*

coloured grey
A grey produced by mixing complementary
colours, eg red and green, blue and orange.

complementary colour
A colour which has the maximum contrast with
another colour. A complementary colour is
produced by mixing two primary colours: eg
green (blue and yellow) is the complementary
colour of red; orange (red and yellow) is the
complementary colour of blue.

composition
The organisation of form in a work of art.

crackle
The surface of a painting when broken by a
network of cracks.

crayon
A stick of coloured drawing material made of
dry pigment and chalk held together with gum
tragacath. Crayons are the drawing medium of
pastel. Wax sticks sold as crayons are thus
incorrectly marketed.

dead colouring: see *underpainting*

distemper
Paint made from water, coloured powders and
size. This is often used for murals when
permanence is not required.

dragging
A method of laying on pigment mixed with little
or no vehicle by dragging it lightly over the
sticky surface of a painting. This produces an
effect of broken colour.

drier: see *siccative*

dry brush
A technique used in drawing, watercolour and
oil painting when a little colour is put on a
brush and then skimmed over the surface.

emulsion
A vehicle made of water and oil with an
emulsifying agent such as casein, egg, etc.

esquisse: see *sketch*

eye level
In perspective the horizon line on which
receding parallel lines meet at a vanishing
point.

fixative
A thin, colourless solution which is sprayed
onto a drawing to prevent smudging.

foreshortening
Using the rules of perspective to create an

illusion of depth and three-dimensionality.

fugitive pigment
Pigment that either fades when exposed to light, reacts to atmospheric pollution, or darkens when mixed with other substances.

gesso
Plaster of Paris or gypsum. Used in tempera painting and also in a mixture of gypsum, size and water.

gouache
A painting medium composed of opaque pigments in a water base.

grisaille
A monochrome painting in shades of grey.

ground
In painting, a coating suitable for receiving pigment. It is applied to the canvas or other support.

hatching
The creation of tonal effects by the use of closely spaced parallel lines. Another set of lines crossing the first at an angle is called cross-hatching.

horizon line
The line where the sky and earth appear to meet. All vanishing points are located on this line.

hue: see *colour*

illusionism
Using optical principles to create an illusion of reality in a painted object. Among the techniques are perspective, foreshortening and chiaroscuro.

impasto
A very heavy or thick application of paint, often showing the marks of a brush, palette knife or other tool. Also called loaded brush or pastose.

imprimatura
A coloured ground or thin, coloured undertint on an outline or preliminary drawing.

intensity: see *colour*

lean colour
Pigment with little oil.

lean surface
A matte surface made by painting with a minimum of oil, especially in underpainting.

line drawing
Drawing in which the main element of definition is line.

linear perspective
The means of delineating three-dimensional objects on a picture plane by drawing them in terms of receding planes.

loaded brush: see *impasto*

local colour
Method of representing the colour of an object

by its hue, then adding shade or lightness using black or white pigment.

matte surface
A dull, flat surface.

medium
The physical materials of which a work of art is made: paint, clay, wood, pastel, ink, gouache, etc. Also used synonymously with 'vehicle' to mean the diluent in which pigment is suspended.

oiling out
A process of rubbing a drying oil (eg linseed oil) over colours which have lost their lustre. Although brilliance is restored, ultimately the effect is to darken them.

oil paint
Paint made by mixing pigment with a drying oil. Linseed oil is the most traditional.

optical mixing
The involuntary mixing of neighbouring colours by the eye and brain. Thus juxtaposed, red and yellow may appear orange. The colours produced by this effect are often more brilliant than those made by mixing colours on a palette.

overpainting
A layer of paint applied over an underlayer.

passage
A term used in referring to a particular area of a painting. It is also used to describe the change from one tone to another, or the use of a special technique, or an area overpainted by another artist.

pastel
A picture executed with sticks formed of coloured powders mixed with gum tragacanth.

pastose: see *impasto*

permanent pigment
Pigment which rarely deteriorates when atmospheric conditions are controlled.

perspective
The technique of representing three-dimensional objects in two dimensions so that they look natural.

picture plane
The surface area of a painting.

pigment
Coloured matter that is mixed with a vehicle to make paint. Can be opaque, translucent or transparent, either permanent or fugitive.

polymer tempera
A synthetic painting medium using a base of polyvinyl acetate or acrylic resin. It is compatible with water, sticks to most surfaces and dries quickly.

poster paint
An opaque watercolour, cheap and therefore fairly fugitive. Also called powder colour or poster colour.

primary colours
Red, yellow and blue. Primary colours can not be made from other colours but all other colours are made from mixing primary colours.

priming
Usually refers to a layer of white which is laid onto a sized canvas in preparation of painting.

pyroxylin
A synthetic medium, often known as lacquer or by a trade name. It is thinned like lacquer and can be used either thickly or thinly.

recession
The illusion of depth in a picture, produced by foreshortening and the use of various techniques of perspective.

relining
The mounting of a painting with its original canvas onto a new canvas support.

retreating colours
Colours which are cool and do not come to the fore, eg blue.

saturation
The degree of brilliance of a colour.

scaling
The flaking-off of paint from the ground, resulting from careless priming or mixing of pigment and varnish, the rolling or folding of the canvas, or dampness affecting the back.

scumble
Applying a thin layer of opaque colour over an underlayer so that the two layers produce a softened effect.

secondary colours
Orange, green and purple: colours made by mixing any two primary colours in equal measures.

shade
The dark degree of a colour or the degree of its brilliance or luminosity. In a picture, the areas representing the absence of light.

siccative
A preparation which, when added to pigments, oils or varnishes, speeds up the drying.

sinking in
The dull matte quality of an oil painting when the pigment is absorbed by the ground.

size
A weak, gelatinous glue used for filling the pores of a canvas, paper, etc., before applying the medium.

sketch
A drawing, painting or model used as a rough draft of the finished composition.

squaring up
A method of transferring a small sketch to a larger surface by dividing it into squares. The same number of squares is then reproduced on the larger surface and the design in the smaller square is copied in the larger square.

stand oil
Linseed oil boiled with the exclusion of air. When thinned and used in paint, it creates an enamel-like smooth finish.

stippling
A method of watercolouring which became popular in the 19th century. The design was made up of very small dots of colour.

stretcher
A wooden frame on which the canvas support is stretched.

support
The untreated surface to which paint is applied after priming. It may be canvas, wood, cardboard, wall, etc.

tempera
A painting material in which the pigment (dissolved in water) is mixed with an albuminous, gelatinous or colloidal medium. The most common tempera vehicle is egg yolk.

tint: see *colour*

tone
In painting, describes the quality of a hue or degree of light and shade.

toning
The tinting of the monochrome underpainting of oil paintings with scumble or glaze.

tooth
The coarseness or grain of the support, i.e. paper, canvas, etc.

underpainting
The first painting of a picture in monochrome to establish the general composition. Also called 'dead painting'.

value: see *colour*

vanishing point
In perspective, the point on the horizon line at which receding parallel lines meet, and seem to vanish.

vehicle
Materials that bind and carry pigments in suspension, usually gum or water, water and egg yolk, or oil.

wash
A thin layer of watercolour or ink, usually on large areas.

watercolour
A pigment with a water soluble binder, such as gum arabic, and dissolved in a water vehicle. A transparent technique in which the highlights are provided by the paper.

yellowing
The discoloration of an oil painting, often because of excessive use of oil, improper siccative or glaze, or damp conditions.

A full range of Rowney painting materials is available from the following suppliers in the United Kingdom:

LONDON
George Rowney & Co Ltd,
Retail Showroom, 12 Percy Street, W1
Cass Arts & Craftsmith,
13 Charing Cross Road, WC2
Green & Stone Ltd,
259 Kings Road, Chelsea, SW3
Harrods,
Knightsbridge, SW1

SOUTH
Artworker,
9 Gunn Street, Reading, Berks
Artworker,
153 Ewell Road, Surbiton, Surrey
Artworker,
15–17 Middle Street, Brighton, Sussex
Artworker,
76 Lee Street, Horley, Surrey
O. W. Annetts,
159 High Street, Sutton, Surrey
A. Boville Wright,
128 High Street, Uxbridge, Middx
A. Boville Wright,
49 Queens Street, Maidenhead, Berks
A. Boville Wright,
Station Road, Gerrards Cross, Bucks
Brush & Compass Ltd,
14 Broad Street, Oxford
Owen Clark Ltd,
133 Cranbrook Road, Ilford, Essex
The Compleat Artist,
102 Crane Street, Salisbury, Wilts
Cass Arts & Craftsmith,
216/8 Marlowes, Hemel Hempstead, Herts
Cass Arts & Craftsmith,
18 George Street, Richmond, Surrey
Cass Arts & Craftsmith,
170 High Street, Slough, Berks
Hampshire Graphics,
175 West Street, Fareham, Hants
Southern Graphics Centre,
176 Upper Elmers End Road, Beckenham, Kent
Avon Graphics,
Colston Centre, Colston Avenue, Bristol, Avon
Dorset Graphic Centre,
24–30 Station Road, Lower Parkstone, Poole, Dorset
E. W. Crump,
61 Burgate, Canterbury, Kent
Fareham Gallery,
162 West Street, Fareham, Hants
Andrew Glass Ltd,
14 Church Street, Reigate, Surrey
H. Hockey,
170–174 White Ladies Road, Bristol, Avon
Harper & Tunstall,
57 Park Street, Bristol, Avon
W. Heffer & Sons,
19 Sydney Street, Cambridge
Francis Iles,
La Providence, High Street, Rochester, Kent

Mawnan Smith,
Fisherman's Lot, West Wharf, Mevagissey, Cornwall
W. G. Morley,
39 Church Street, Croydon, Surrey
The Picture Shop,
44–46 Church Street, Weybridge, Surrey
The Picture Shop (Thomas Fine Arts),
41 West Road, Hove, Sussex
Sussex Stationers Ltd,
10 East Street, Brighton
Sussex Stationers Ltd,
27 George Street, Hove
Sussex Stationers Ltd,
34–35 High Street, Lewes
Sussex Stationers Ltd,
105 Montague Street, Worthing
Sussex Stationers Ltd,
16 Terminus Road, Eastbourne
Sussex Stationers Ltd,
10 Wellington Place, Hastings
Trinity Gallery,
Trinity Street, Colchester, Essex

MIDLANDS
W. F. Gadsby,
22 Market Place, Leicester
Graphic Link,
5–8 End Dale, Birmingham
Harper & Tunstall,
13 Cannon Street, Birmingham
Sisson & Parker Ltd,
25 Wheeler Gate, Nottingham

EAST ANGLIA
Jarrolds Ltd,
London Street, Norwich
Jarrolds Ltd,
182 Kings Street, Great Yarmouth

NORTH & NORTH-EAST
G. D. Andrews,
4 Holly Lane, Sheffield
Arts & Crafts,
10 Byram Street, Huddersfield
James Dinsdale Ltd,
King Charles Street, Leeds
W. F. Gadsby,
33 New Briggate, Leeds
Granthams,
Charnley Road, Blackpool
Granthams,
70 North Gate, Blackburn
Granthams,
Friargate, Preston
Hibbert Brothers,
117 Norfolk Street, Sheffield
Thornes Bookshop,
63–67 Percy Street, Newcastle-upon-Tyne
Thornes Bookshop,
165 Lindthorpe Road, Middlesborough

SCOTLAND
Miller's Graphic Centre,
54 Queen Street, Glasgow
John Mathieson,
48 Frederick Street, Edinburgh

INDEX

Picture Credits

The publisher would like to thank the following who have supplied pictures and photographs:
Charlotte Avery: 15 (top).
Laurence Bradbury: 27, 30 (bottom), 40, 109.
Sue Branch: 12, 30 (top), 52–3, 102–3, 119, 122, 126–7, 149.
Terence Brind: 78.
French Government Tourist Office: 14.
Peter Harrison: 91, 123.
Ingrid Jacob: 42–3.
Francis Lumley: 22, 23, 58–9, 105, 108, 128.
Ronald Pearsall: 132–3.
Shirley Read: 176–7.
George Rowney & Co Ltd: 11, 60–1, 66–7, 70–1, 106–7, 143, 158–9.
Royal Academy of Arts: 180–1.
Dennis Ryan: 19, 134–5, 138–9, 142, 144–5, 146–7, 148, 150–1, 154–5, 160–1, 162–3, 166–7.
Peter Seddon: 110–11, 112–13, 114–15, 118, 120–1, 124–5.
Peter Stanyer: 26, 28, 31, 62–3, 65, 74–5, 80–1, 82–3, 86, 90, 164–5, 169.
John Tetley: 17.
Gordon Thompson: 41, 44–5.
Michael Webb: 16, 21, 24–5, 29, 32, 39, 84–5, 88–9.
Roy Williams: 68–9, 170–1, 172–3, 174–5, 179, 182–3.
Hon C. Wong: 33 (bottom), 34–5, 36–7, 38, 46, 48–9.

Thanks also to N. Mann, picture framers, Monmouth Street, London WC2, for their kind cooperation.

Line drawings by Malcolm Brown
Front cover: Peter Seddon, Peter Stanyer, Dennis Ryan
Back cover: Peter Stanyer